T0065526

Belmont:
The Billion Dollar High School

FIGHTING FRAUD & WASTE IN
SCHOOL CONSTRUCTION

DON MULLINAX
WITH LESLIE DUTTON & TJ JOHNSTON
OF FULL DISCLOSURE NETWORK

authorHOUSE°

AuthorHouse™
1663 Liberty Drive
Bloomington, IN 47403
www.authorhouse.com
Phone: 833-262-8899

Published by AuthorHouse 11/04/2020

ISBN: 978-1-6655-0368-6 (sc)
ISBN: 978-1-6655-0370-9 (hc)
ISBN: 978-1-6655-0369-3 (e)

Library of Congress Control Number: 2020920052

Print information available on the last page.

This book is printed on acid-free paper.

CONTENTS

FOREWORD

Responsible parents teach their children that lying is a bad thing. But then kids figure out quickly that there are negative consequences *only if* they are caught not telling the truth. Children, of course, grow up. And they continue to lie into adulthood for one of two basic reasons---to receive rewards or to avoid punishment (or a combination of both).

Fraud is a special kind of lie. It involves depriving others of money or property by making false statements. There is no such thing as an "accidental" fraud. Under common law, fraud---no matter what type---involves four basic elements: (1) a material false statement; (2) knowledge that the statement was false when uttered; (3) reliance by the victim(s) on the falsehood; and (4) damages as a result.

I have over four decades' experience in the anti-fraud profession. Beginning as an auditor for a large accounting firm, I then spent ten years with the Federal Bureau of Investigation specializing in the detection and deterrence of white-collar crime. Thereafter, I helped start what is now the world's largest anti-fraud association with members in over 150 nations. It was in that capacity that I met Don Mullinax, this book's author.

Don, a true expert in the field, knows that the deck is stacked against us when trying to bring fraudsters to the bar of justice. To begin, the U.S. system assumes the innocence of those charged unless and until it can be proven otherwise. Convicting someone of a crime was intentionally made difficult by the framers of the Constitution.

Moreover, frauds must compete with other crimes for the limited resources and crowded dockets of the criminal justice system. Prosecutors, every day, must decline pursuing cases because the system is already so overloaded. The frauds that tend to be investigated are the simple ones where proof is easy; or alternatively, frauds so large (and often so complex) that ignoring them would be a miscarriage of justice.

It is with this background that Don Mullinax, Certified Fraud Examiner, was tasked to investigate what could have been the most expensive possible fraud in the history of Los Angeles County, California---a high school complex built directly over abandoned, early 20th Century oil fields. Originally estimated at around $100 million to construct, the local taxpayers would eventually shell out nearly ten times that amount. Yes, nearly a billion dollars spent, and millions wasted because those involved did not make the right decisions the first time.

Don and his team took almost three years for what was dubbed as the "Belmont investigation." They interviewed nearly 350 witnesses, examined over 8,800 pages of building plans and inspected 1,100 boxes of documents, all in a futile effort to prove criminal fraud; there were no charges, indictments or convictions in the end. But there were valuable learning lessons.

The first is that the author shows you a textbook approach to conducting a fraud examination; it is not easy. The second lesson is how unique fraud cases are from other offenses. In a theft, the major question is *who* committed the crime. But in a fraud, the identity of a suspect is almost always known, and the question is: does the *conduct* constitute a crime?

Many times, there are no clear answers. In my own experience of conducting over a thousand investigations, only about a quarter of them led to charges. But that certainly does not mean the time was wasted. Fraud is less likely to be attempted when people like Don Mullinax (and you and I) are on the lookout.

Dr. Joseph T. Wells, CFE, CPA
Founder and Chairman
Association of Certified Fraud Examiners
Austin, Texas

PREFACE

Many people may ask, why write a book 20 years after your report on the Belmont Learning Complex ("Belmont") was issued? The answer is very simple – the media reports almost weekly about fraud, waste, and mismanagement of school construction and modernization programs from California to New York and in many states in between. These media reports highlight many of the same poor management practices and processes that we found during our investigation of Belmont – the nation's most expensive high school. So, the findings and lessons learned from Belmont are still relevant today. The purpose of this book is to provide citizens, parents, and school officials across the country with a useful tool that will hopefully help them not make the same mistakes as those who came before them.

Another question that I'm often asked is, how did you determine that Belmont's cost was $1 billion when most media reports highlight the price was approximately $400 million? Again, a simple answer. It appears that the $400 million that has been used by the media was provided by the Los Angeles Unified School District ("LAUSD"). Based on my personal experience of over six years working with and examining the LAUSD's financial systems, one cannot rely on the numbers that its financial and accounting systems generated. Up until the time that the Belmont project was restarted in 2005, the

LAUSD did not have an acceptable project cost accounting system. As such, many costs associated with the Belmont project were not recorded, tracked, and reported.

For example, the costs associated with the:

(i)   hours that LAUSD staff spent on the Belmont project,

(ii)   demolition of existing structures that did not meet building codes,

(iii)   removal of air conditioning units and other equipment that had sit idle and were inoperable, and

(iv)   interest on the revenue bonds or often referred to as Certificates of Participation (which was hundreds of million dollars alone). As a result, if the LAUSD's reported cost of the Belmont project is $400 million, I believe that the actual price is at least two or three times higher or closer to $1 billion.

If you take nothing else away from reading this book, please focus on and use the 10 takeaways in the final chapter to help you follow the right path to implementing and maintaining a high-performance school facilities construction and modernization program.

CHAPTER 1

A Long Way from Georgia

I was born in Ellijay, Georgia – a small city in the foothills of the Appalachian Mountains. The name "Ellijay" was taken from the Cherokee word "Elatse' Yi meaning "new ground" or "green earth." When I say small city, I mean small – a population of 1,500 covering 3.5 square miles with one traffic light, and four schools (1 high school and three elementary schools).

Growing up in this small-town setting did not prepare me for the size of the Los Angeles Unified School District (LAUSD) –second-largest school district in the U.S. covering 720 square miles with over 1,300 schools and education centers. And if those numbers were not staggering enough – how about almost 1 million students with a $6 billion annual budget and $20 billion school construction and modernization program. Maybe I should have stayed in Ellijay.

It was a pretty simple and straight forward phone call from the LAUSD School Board – I think it came from Board Member David Tokofsky. "We want you to initiate a review of Belmont." I was in the middle of rebuilding the disaster of an office and a staff of people who were lost and leaderless that I had inherited when I signed on with the LAUSD. I really didn't need any additional projects, especially a highly visible and politically sensitive one, at the time. *Who is this Belmont character*, I asked? Little did I know, the monstrosity simply called Belmont would consume my life for the next three years.

David Tokofsky
LAUSD Board Member

Being the "new guy" at LAUSD, I wasn't about to drag my feet. Janet Eiler and I were the only real investigators in the school district's newly created Office of Internal Audit and Special Investigations (later renamed Office of Inspector General). Sure, I had inherited a staff of almost 30 people, but some of them struggled with performing simple audits of cafeteria funds and payroll, let alone conducting a major investigation of a multimillion-dollar construction project. According to the auditing firm KPMG, which had been hired by LAUSD, the office I had adopted was dysfunctional. It was leaderless and hopeless. My priority was to get it whipped into shape. I always try to maintain a positive attitude. So, I became determined to turn this burdensome task into an opportunity. I saw this new Belmont task as a means to get the staff and budget I needed to run a first-class Office of Inspector General for the school district.

It was what I was good at. I had just come from the big time of Washington D.C. politics. I had served as the Chief Investigator of the U.S. Senate Permanent Subcommittee on Investigations. I worked with Senator Collins from Maine on major investigations of healthcare fraud, public corruption, and food safety. I helped write position papers for Senator Collins and helped draft legislation, resulting in landmark bills such as S.1231, the "Medicare Fraud Prevention and Enforcement

Act of 1999". As a Certified Fraud Examiner, I developed a reputation that I was a "hardball reformer." My driving mission was to protect our nation from the unscrupulous who would take advantage of the river of money flowing through the Federal Government. As Chief Investigator, my job also was to monitor and provide oversight of approximately 70 Federal Offices of Inspector General to make sure that they had adequate funding and staffing to perform their essential role of conducting audits and investigations.

But my mother-in-law was having health issues. And my wife wanted to live closer to Hawaii and not half the world away. And I was getting tired of the non-stop lifestyle of constant politics in Washington, D.C. Although I got a little break by playing softball with the U.S. Senate Softball League with my lawyer pal James Kawahara, the constant eruption of never-ending issues was taking over my entire life. I needed to escape the boiling pot of the Nation's Capital. So, in the summer of 1998, I saw a vacancy announcement in the Los Angeles Times for a Director of Investigative Audits at the LAUSD. I sent in my resume.

In July 1998, Ann Young (a representative of LAUSD's Human Resources Department) contacted me to set up a 40-minute phone interview. I thought it went very well until I received a letter a month later from Ms. Young notifying me that two of the five candidates were moving forward to an interview with the LAUSD's Audit Committee and that I was not one of those two candidates. I should have foreseen what was going to happen next.

Out of the blue, on September 11, 1998, Ms. Young called me to say that the Audit Committee had requested to interview (in person) all five of the prior candidates. For reasons beyond my comprehension, I was back in the running. I immediately booked a flight to Los Angeles.

On September 28th, I met with the cast of characters that would frustrate my life for the next decade. I interviewed with four LAUSD Board Members: Victoria Castro, Jeff Horton, Julie Korenstein, and David Tokofsky, along with a person from the Human Resources Department and an external member.

I learned a lot from the interview. It seems that they lacked any financial controls with no ability to account for who was spending millions of taxpayers' dollars. The School Board had hired the audit firm of KPMG to evaluate LAUSD's Internal Audit Branch. The report came back as a scathing indictment of their operation. KPMG recommended combining both LAUSD's internal audit and investigative functions into one "Internal Audit and Special Investigations Unit."

I felt the interview went exceedingly well. I was confident I hit it out of the park. I got the impression that Board Member David Tokofsky was trying to set up an Office of Inspector General for LAUSD — what I considered my specialty. Obviously, from the report from its auditing firm, the LAUSD management had no way of knowing where its money was going and who was spending it on what. And this was a school district with an annual budget of over 6 billion dollars! I fielded Mr. Tokofsky's questions — knowing what he needed, and I felt sure I could do what was necessary to get LAUSD the accountability it so sorely needed. If I got the job, I was going to shine, I just knew it.

In mid-December, I was officially offered the position of Director, Internal Audit and Special Investigations Unit (the position was later renamed Inspector General). I agreed to report to work in Los Angeles on January 19, 1999 – a day that would forever change my life.

CHAPTER 2

Day 1

I flew into the LAX Airport the weekend before my start date and found a room at the Omni Hotel. I had heard of it from the "Trial of the Century" — the OJ Simpson trial, and it was where the jury had been sequestered. I reasoned that the jury to the most prominent media trial in U.S. history wouldn't stay at some dump. And I appreciated that it was within walking distance of the KPMG Building where I was to report to my office. Although it was close and convenient, it wasn't cheap. I started looking for an apartment right away. In the meantime, my wife would start making arrangements to sell our D.C. home.

So bright and early, at 8 a.m. on January 19, 1999, I reported to work at LAUSD. I reported in at the 450 North Grand office, which was the headquarters of the school district. Because the LAUSD Headquarters building didn't have enough space to house the Internal Audit and Special Investigations Unit, my office would be at the KPMG building – the same KPMG whose auditors had written the damning report that resulted in me being hired.

A few days earlier, I had received a phone call from Stephanie Johnson of KPMG to let me know what I was getting into. Stephanie had been keeping the District auditing office running until I arrived.

Now she was washing her hands of the mess. I must admit, I became concerned when I heard in her voice the welcomed relief she felt as she handed off the baton.

When I arrived at the LAUSD Headquarters, I reported to the office of Roger Rasmussen, Director of the Independent Analysis Unit, who assisted me with in-processing and took me to meet Superintendent Dr. Ruben Zacarias, Chief Administrative Officer David Koch, and LAUSD Board President Vicki Castro.

I must admit liking Vicki. She was a no-nonsense, get 'er done kind of person. During our initial pleasantries, she discovered I had walked to the office. I wasn't concerned about walking. That was just standard practice on the East Coast. Apparently not so in Southern California. She ordered Jefferson Crain, the Board Secretariat, to "get Don a car" among the first action items we discussed. She was a "mover and shaker." In a significant way, she had been responsible for the passage of Proposition BB in April 1997 – the $2.4 billion bond to repair school buildings – the first and largest bond approved by voters in more than 20 years. Sadly, these funds were to be sucked into the black hole known as Belmont.

After a brief meeting, I headed over to the KPMG building to meet my staff. Surprisingly Ms. Castro went with me. In fact, she drove.

We crowded everybody together in the KPMG conference room. There were 35 people jammed in there. They were all impressed with the "Big Guns" addressing them. It was the first time any of the audit staff had ever met the school board President. I was impressed. Their presence showed that I was going to be well-supported in my efforts to reform this sadly under-performing office. I was pleased to have the backing. Little did I know how hard it would be to get this warm, fuzzy kind of support just a year later.

I quickly took charge of the meeting and made introductions. I identified what I expected of them and what they could expect of me. The blank stares I noted around the room made me realize that this department was in far more trouble than I had hoped. I always try to be positive and optimistic, but what I saw in front of me confirmed what I expected from the KPMG audit report. I was now positive that the vast majority of the staff could handle only minor tasks such as auditing a cafeteria budget or student body funds. They had no comprehension of how to investigate purchase order fraud or contract billing schemes.

I had to find out exactly what I had to work with, so I began meetings with each individual of my inherited audit staff and also the District senior staff, including the CFO, the controller, the Business Services Manager, Lynn Roberts, who was in charge of the Proposition BB Bond Program, and especially Elizabeth Louargand, the Facilities Manager.

I needed help in a hurry. The school board wanted a status report ASAP. I figured I had about three weeks before the new-guy shine would be gone. There was a lump in my gut like I had swallowed a large boulder, just sitting there, indigestible. What had I gotten myself into?

The problem was patience. LAUSD was getting hammered by the local media. They had passed this huge bond measure, and the school district seemed to be hemorrhaging money. Tony Anderson, a partner from Ernst & Young and an outside member of the audit committee, was pressuring the LAUSD Board — based upon KPMG report — to eliminate the entire Audit and Investigations department and outsource everything. According to him, "the staff people aren't trained, and aren't qualified; the district could save a bundle of money by outsourcing." As he related it, the entire office was a black eye for school district.

The pressure was intense right from day one. I pleaded with Ms. Castro – give me some time to turn this situation around. I seemed to get a reprieve for a while. Little did I know, behind the scenes, they were preparing a significant School Board resolution to begin a review of the Belmont Learning Complex.

CHAPTER 3

My "Dream Team"

The media was slamming LAUSD about something called "Belmont." Board Members (including Valerie Fields, Julie Korenstein, George Kiriyama, and Vicki Castro), one after another began calling me regarding a proposal to investigate Belmont. I'd never heard of it. I cornered Board Member Valerie Fields and Jeff Crain (the Executive Secretary for the School Board) and asked them to give me a quick low-down on this Belmont situation. They let me know it was a new high school LAUSD was trying to build. It was going to be a new concept of design-build, just a couple blocks down the street.

This new project would feature not only a school, but a retail component, and a housing component. It was a new model called a "joint venture," where the school was to be funded by the other parts. The school district was hard-pressed to fund a new school. None had been built in the last 25 years, and kids were being bussed all over the 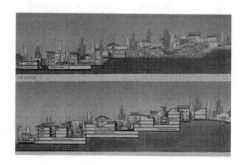 county, so this new school was desperately needed. The concept was brought to the school district by a developer: Wayne Wedin.

In February 1981, barely one month after retiring from his 15-year career as Brea City Manager and Redevelopment Agency

Director, Wayne Wedin went to work consulting for the Brea-Olinda School District. During the next four years, Wedin made $323,000 in consulting fees for a project remarkably similar to what was being proposed for Belmont – build a commercial development on site to pay for a new school. That plan in Brea would have worked beautifully had the site for the new school been something other than an abandoned oil field — a site never tested for environmental damage and toxicity.

Then it hit. On February 23, 1999, the LAUSD School Board directed my newly formed team, the "Office of Internal Audit and Special Investigations Unit" to investigate the following six issues regarding Belmont:

1. The acquisition, environmental assessment, and remediation of all land associated with Belmont;
2. All contracts and payments to outside consultants and attorneys involved with Belmont;
3. Alleged existences of conflicts of interest relating to Belmont;
4. Any account controlled by the former Bond an Asset Management/Planning and Development offices;
5. The selection, negotiation, and contracting process for the development and construction of Belmont; and
6. Pursue all legal rights and remedies, including restitution in the event of the discovery of any wrongdoing regarding Belmont.

Oh boy, I probably should have been gravely concerned, knowing what I know today. But these were dynamite marching orders. I was charged up. I had my assignment. It was clear: identify the problems, identify all those responsible, and hold them accountable.

But now, I began to understand the scope of the project. I needed a lot more help. I knew I would need qualified investigators. So, I started calling some of my old investigator contacts back in Washington, D.C. I contacted my old friends Don Wheeler and Eric Eskew looking for "detailees" to aid in investigations. They informed me they could not detail federal employees to local government offices.

So, I called my old friend James Kawahara, who had recently moved from Washington and was now residing in Los Angeles. He was on board with Preston Gates & Ellis. I called James to assist with legal matters. When the detailee pursuit didn't work out, I began searching on the Internet for experienced former or retired FBI agents that did investigative work. That's when I found Wayne Owens of Owens & Associates Investigations, who was able to put me in touch with many of the talented individuals who became my outside investigators.

At the same time, Doug Smith of the Los Angeles Times and Eric Moses of the L.A. Daily News began calling me inquiring about the pending investigation. The local Los Angeles papers printed a story based on the authorization by the School Board. It went nationwide: "Mullinax going to lead a major investigation of Belmont."

The phones exploded. I got hundreds of responses, and it took hundreds of long hours to sort out the quality from the riffraff. I got inquiries from major firms such as Arthur Andersen, Kroll Associates, and Public Investigations, Inc., along with several local law firms. To hire all these people, I had to convert existing vacant positions into contract dollars. It took some wrangling with the

Human Resources Department, but I got it done. I was delighted with the team of heavy hitters I assembled.

At Preston Gates & Ellis, along with my trusted friend James, I contracted attorneys Roger Carrick, David Sadwick, and Angela Dotson as well as legal assistants Beto Chavez and Lee Paige. I also recruited a slew of investigators including former FBI special agents Wayne Owens, Fred Ahles, William Fleming, Joseph Chefalo, Jack Orswell, Michael Walt, Robert Taylor, Norman Wight, and Darwin Wisdom. And I was especially pleased to hire forensic accountants Ralph Summerford, Kelly Todd, and Lisa Robins of Summerford Accountancy, PC (subsequently named Forensic Strategic Solutions), and also an expert in environmental science and policy, David Leu, Ph. D from the Leu Group.

This was my "Dream Team," and we were primed and ready to go on the hunt. I assembled our first kick-off meeting on March 19, 1999. The Belmont investigation was officially happening.

CHAPTER 4

The Uphill Battle Begins

As I entered the meeting room, the air was alive with electricity. I knew from my long years as an investigator that I had assembled the "best of the best." There were almost 20 people in the room, all seasoned professionals. As we went around the room, with everybody introducing themselves, I was impressed by the talent in front of me — including former white-collar crime investigators from the FBI.

Then it was my turn. I introduced myself and explained the scope of work. We were to investigate this school building project known as the "Belmont Learning Complex." Our immediate task was to develop a list of documents that would explain what had happened to date. And then we needed to create a witness list – people that could tell us what they said, what they did, and where the bodies were buried. And then there was the deadline. We had to give the School Board a report on our findings within six months. There were some grim faces in front of me but determined.

We brainstormed for several hours, deciding who would pursue which angles. Anticipating the massive quantity of documents, we expected, we had to come up with a unique and an entirely new way to index and file all the hundreds of pages we knew we were about to receive. The data retrieval system had to identify the persons, places, and subjects in an electronic database that would help us link all the variables of the information to establish cause and effect. And then, it would need to identify where that specific document was stored so we could access it at will. Our computer geniuses were challenged with this task. They set up the document storage at the law firm of Preston Gates & Ellis, where they thought they would have enough space. Boy, were they wrong!

And so, we drafted a couple of memorandums to request all documents. On March 26, 1999, we sent out our written request for all Belmont-related documents. These requests went to the LAUSD Chief Administrative Officer David Koch and Chief Financial Officer Olonzo Woodfin asking for their full cooperation.

The silence was deafening. Although all the key figures within LAUSD had made solemn and public statements pledging their full cooperation, the reality was anything but cooperative. Some of the school district staff completely ignored the request letters.

Obviously, from their past experiences with the office of the Internal Auditor, they had no respect for our mission and our authority. When we leaned on some of the senior staff, they were openly defensive and completely uncooperative. So, on June 14, 1999, I sent

a letter to School Board President Vicki Castro and Superintendent Ruben Zacarias requesting their assistance in getting staff to provide documents. And we also began having our former FBI guys visit staff offices to put a little more pressure on folks.

We finally began to get responses. We got tons of stuff: dozens and dozens of boxes of files. Every day another shipment would come in. Our investigators began digging through the documents and discovered they were being buried in mostly useless junk. Apparently, the LAUSD staff had said, "You want documents? Here's your stinking documents!" and tossed everything with the slightest reference to the Belmont project into a box – unsorted and with no information about what the documents referred to and no information about what was in the box. They sealed it up nice and neat, and then defiantly shipped it to us. "Take that!" we could hear their thinking, as each box hit the floor at Preston Gates & Ellis.

Undaunted, my staff combed through the mountains of papers, date stamping, coding, indexing, and storing each sheet so that, in the case that some gem of information was relevant, we would be able to retrieve it.

At the same time, we began our interviews. Over the ensuing six months of investigations, we interviewed more than 65 individuals. Many of them several times. We developed a unique script that we would recite before starting the interview. It was intended to set the interviewee at ease, but I'm sure that many of our witnesses felt like suspects being given a Miranda warning. Many times, the subject of our interviews would question whether they needed a lawyer or their union representative. Although it wasn't intentional, I guess we were quite intimidating.

The investigation into the Belmont Learning Complex had begun in earnest. It was a massive, exhausting, demanding, and frustrating task. But slowly and surely, we started to see the project take shape. As we looked over the vast piles of paper and listened to the witnesses, we began to see a vague form of the project. With our excellent investigators, we began to see the potential problems that perhaps were the cause of the fiasco.

Progress was slow and tedious. And we had to fight for every piece of evidence. The resistance was unrelenting. In fact, just nine days before we released our first report, we received six boxes of Belmont-related documents from the General Counsel (Richard Mason) that he said he "just happened to locate" – six months after our initial request. It was going to be an uphill fight all the way to the top.

CHAPTER 5

The Media Smelt Blood

After the School Board had passed the resolution authorizing the investigation of the Belmont Learning Complex, the media smelled blood in the water. I received a slew of phone calls inquiring about me, the new personnel I had on board, and the direction of our investigation.

The media had been pounding on the School Board for months. Paraphrasing Sandra Dunn of L.A. Weekly when she asked, "How are you going to conduct a decent investigation in light of KPMG's blistering report saying that the audit department was totally dysfunctional?" I knew I was being tested as well. "Will the new kid roll over?" "Will this new Director be as inept as the former Director?" I could feel everyone's eyes on me, but having dealt with the media many times in Washington, D.C., I thought I could handle the situation.

On January 28, 1999, I met with Doug Smith of the L.A. Times. We had a nice lunch meeting at the Taipan Restaurant. Doug was very forthcoming with information. He had served as a de facto "Hotline" for LAUSD employees who wanted to report shenanigans within the school district but had no place to file their grievances. Doug and I came to an understanding. I would listen to his input and follow up on it. I would provide him with my audit reports, which I also published on the Internet. But I made sure that he understood that I could not share any information regarding our Belmont investigation before it was published. I needed to make sure that nothing leaked out.

California State Senator Tom Hayden was pushing for subpoena authority for the Internal Audit and Investigations Unit. Until we got it, we had to make sure that no one knew what direction we were going, so information that we were seeking would not "disappear." The element of surprise was our most important tool: that, and the power of intimidation.

The interviews we conducted were not the same as the typical audits from LAUSD. I now had a staff of seasoned former FBI investigators, who were professionals at investigating white-collar crime. They knew how to read body language. They knew how to follow up with hard questions. They knew how to corner a lie and force the interviewee to admit any contradictions. Add to this with the fact that we threatened to publish openly any lack of cooperation. We were playing hardball. This was unheard of within the LAUSD.

I was very pleased with the integrity of my team. I had threatened to terminate anybody who leaked anything to the media. As a result, we never had any leaks to the press. Within the LAUSD, this was a stunning change. The LAUSD was known for its leaks. This secrecy allowed us the opportunity to interview witnesses without tipping our hand where we wanted the interview to go. It was a real plus to have that tight control of what was given to the press and the School Board, and what wasn't.

I was the sole source of information for the Internal Audit and Special Investigations Unit. As a result, not only did I report to the School Board, but I would carefully control the amount of information given to the media. I believe in open transparency but wanted to make sure that the wrong comment didn't end up slandering the people involved in Belmont. And so, I was careful in approaching any interview with the media.

Toward the end of 2003, I was interviewed by Leslie Dutton of the Full Disclosure Network. I had been interviewed hundreds of  times before and felt very comfortable going in. Unlike many of the interviewers in the other media, she was exceptionally well prepared. For example, she brought up questions about LAUSD's Financing Corporation, something that had never come up in my Belmont investigation. Apparently, the school district would buy and hold available properties for future expansion. If the school district's Facilities Division needed money, they could sell the property on the open market. It was a separate funding and holding entity within LAUSD, of which I was entirely unaware. And any School Board discussion was always done in closed session. This Financing Corporation was a ripe target for future investigations. And this interview started a long and fruitful relationship.

Ms. Dutton was a "hard charger" as we called her in our office. She would never take "no" for an answer. Striving to make good on the name of her program, Ms. Dutton pursued everybody involved in the Belmont project. She was aggressive but never employed abusive tactics. Ms. Dutton gently offered to air their perspective without edits, and that's how she got them on her show. But once there, she never pulled any punches.

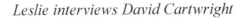

Leslie interviews David Cartwright

I have had the pleasure of watching the dozens of interviews on the Full Disclosure Network. Although Ms. Dutton never took sides, they were always very revealing. Several of the comments in the following chapters are taken directly from those interviews. Sometimes they supported our reports. Sometimes they contradicted our reports. In either case, they helped to complete the picture of utter chaos and confusion that was Belmont. And in most cases, the interviews were quite engaging and entertaining.

The following narrative is the result of our investigations – combined with the in-depth interviews conducted by Ms. Dutton. It is a story of incredible incompetence, with shameful subplots of immense greed and corruption. And all the names are included to make sure the innocent people are protected from them in the future.

CHAPTER 6

A History of Poisoned Ground

In the summer of 1989, an oily substance was found seeping up through the asphalt playground of the Park Avenue Elementary School in Cudahy, California (Cudahy is approximately 10 miles from downtown Los Angeles). The school was closed immediately to investigate the source of the seepage.

The nasty black goo was coming from discarded petroleum products dumped years before in an old landfill, where the Park Avenue School is now located.

This seepage discovery resulted in a public outcry, and California State Senator Art Torres convened a public hearing in Cudahy on August 11, 1989. Senator Torres was the chair of the Senate's Committee on Toxics and Public Safety Management.

At the hearing, a parent, Mr. Ernie Castillo, testified that the LAUSD had known for 20 years that there was a continual seepage. He identified that LAUSD had been given the "Thorn Report" in December 1988. This report had identified five specific carcinogenic materials present under the Park Avenue School.

Mr. Castillo testified that Ms. Susie Wong, the Chief Safety Officer of LAUSD, had, on June 20, 1989, "denied that it was serious enough to do something about it."

California Senator Larry Stirling, the Vice-Chair of the Toxics Committee commented, "I just walked over to the school. You can smell the methane gas emitting from the ground there."

LAUSD was defensive in response. During the hearing, Chairman Torres interviewed David Koch, LAUSD's Administrator of the Business and Services Division.

Torres: Has the School District changed its school siting procedure to avoid buying and building on contaminated property?

Koch: As Assemblyperson Hughes is aware, the District is trying to construct a number of schools because of our overcrowding.

Torres: That's not what I asked. I asked, does the School District plan to revise its procedures in siting and building on contaminated property?

Koch: The Board is trying to weigh the...

Torres: I'm asking whether it will be your recommendation whether the School District should revise its siting procedures to avoid buying and building on contaminated property?

Koch: If the contaminated property can be adequately mitigated, I think it's okay.

Torres: How many present school sites in Los Angeles Unified School District are within a quarter-mile of a dumpsite?

Koch: About thirty-nine.

Torres: Is it your intent or your recommendation that there be significant testing done by an independent agency to determine the nature of those sites that are within a quarter-mile of a school?

Koch: We have to date conducted tests at all these sites.

Torres: At all thirty-nine sites.

Koch: Over two hundred sites. Actually, two hundred thirty some odd sites for methane, because the problem of methane is not limited to landfills. It also occurs in oil fields; it occurs in natural oil foundation and tar pit sort of situations.

And so, before the construction of the Belmont Learning Complex, there was a significantly long history of dealing with contaminated school sites. On her Full Disclosure Network program, Leslie Dutton interviewed Dr. Kaye Kilburn, a noted author, who held the Ralph Edgington Chair, Keck School of Medicine at USC. His most noted book, "Chemical Brain Injury," clearly documented the deadly effects of gases that emanate from any oil field. Dr. Kilburn was intimately aware of the dangers of building a school in Los Angeles:

> "We're Los Angeles. We're an oil field. We were an oil field well before Los Angeles was ever thought of. Go to the tar pits at La Brea and see. So, there's no  way of getting rid of what we sit on. The earth is really the way it is, and it's full of hydrogen sulfide. It's bubbling to the surface, the old boreholes through cracks in the earth from our numerous earthquake patterns and other breaks that have been made. There was a normal bubbling to the surface even before all this, I'm sure."

Regardless, LAUSD was happily going ahead with building hundreds of schools on contaminated property throughout Los Angeles. On August 21, 1989, a mere 10 days after the Park Avenue hearing before Senator Torres, the LAUSD School Board approved the land acquisition program for what was then known as Belmont New Junior High School #1.

LAUSD was not about to be concerned about some lame little hearing conducted by some irritating state senators. They had schools to build and couldn't be bothered by hysterical parents and grandstanding politicians. With eyes firmly shut and ears solidly plugged, they were going full steam ahead on what eventually became the Belmont Learning Complex.

CHAPTER 7

First Street and Beaudry Avenue

LAUSD desperately needed a school in the Belmont region of Los Angeles.

An attorney for the law firm O'Melveny & Myers, David Cartwright, served as the outside counsel for LAUSD. In an interview with the Full Disclosure Network he said:

> "At the time – we're talking now the late '80s and moving into the early '90s – the school district had virtually no money. The State funding was off. There was no bond money like there is now. We have a couple of propositions L.A. Unified has, and superintendents like Bill Anton and Sid Thompson were faced with a situation where the District population was rising 10% a year, or 5%, and there were no new schools. There hadn't been a new high school built in 30 years. This is a problem. Children were being bussed to the Valley, to the Westside, as much as two to three

hours round trip a day. And this particular area in
Belmont, which is near downtown, was a burgeoning
population, frequently of Central American and
Mexican immigrants who might not be registered to
vote and thus didn't have a strong voice. And it was
thousands of kids were getting bussed around, so that
became part of the process, too."

At the same time, during the late eighties, Federal laws were
passed imposing strict liability for landowners of contaminated
property. Law firms advised their developer clients to divest
themselves of these lands to avoid massive liability. So, these major
developers offered deeds instead of foreclosure or eventually let
contaminated properties be foreclosed in attempts to relieve
themselves of liability.

Shimizu, a Japanese construction
corporation (known as S-P
Corporation), found itself saddled
with the property in the vicinity of
First Street and Beaudry Avenue in
downtown Los Angeles. Shimizu
was planning to build a high-density
commercial development named the "Pacific Basin Plaza" as part of
its Central City West development. Shimizu looked at this site as a
significant liability. The land was toxic.

Ed Scott is an oil and gas expert;
his specialty is conducting Phase I site
assessments, which are used to identify
potential or existing environmental
contamination liabilities. In an interview

with the Full Disclosure Network, he described the history of this
area of land:

> "Well, oil fields and these particular oil fields have
> been there for a number of years, since the early 1900s,
>  I believe. There were
> over 1,000 wells on the
> site. Oil wells have a
> tremendous amount of
> equipment on them. They
> use a lot of petroleum
> products to keep that equipment operating. A lot of that
> is spilled on those sites, and so you not only have
> contamination from the oil that is being brought up, but
> you have contamination from petroleum products that
> are already developed that get spilled on the site."

Shimizu saw in LAUSD an easy way to get out of its liability.
Shimizu proposed to develop and construct affordable housing on
the southern part of its property at First Street and Beaudry Avenue.
And then Shimizu promised to make a sweet deal for LAUSD and
sell them the property for their middle school on the northern 11 acres
near Temple Street and Beaudry Avenue.

The school district leaped at this opportunity. On August 26,
1989, the LAUSD Board approved a land acquisition program
for Belmont New Junior High School #1. The Board directed the
LAUSD environmental branch to begin the environmental review
process. Actually, the school district wanted the site at First Street
and Beaudry Avenue but located the junior high site at Temple Street
and Beaudry Avenue. This change was in response to an agreement
(Temple Beaudry Agreement) with commercial developers and

the community not to build on the preferred site. LAUSD began to acquire property on the 11-acre site for aggregate purchase price of $30 million.

But there was a significant problem with the northern 11 acres. It was toxic.

CHAPTER 8

The "Exxon Valdez" Property

The Los Angeles City Oil Field was first developed in the 1890s. The Toluca oil production wells adjacent to the Belmont site have an average depth of 1,000 feet below ground surface, though oil production has been obtained at levels as shallow at 600 feet below ground.

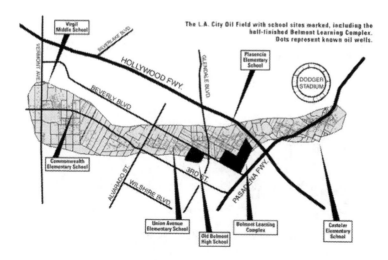

The L.A. City Oil Field with school sites marked, including the half-finished Belmont Learning Complex. Dots represent known oil wells.

Resulting from the embarrassing fiasco of the Park Avenue Elementary School, California State Senator Torres passed legislation (SB2262), which became law January 1, 1990. This new law clarified existing rules regarding the school site selection process, explicitly addressing hazardous sites. This new law required school districts to submit potential sites to the California Department of Conservation, Division of Oil, Gas and Geothermal Resources ("Division of Oil and Gas"). The Division of Oil and Gas would begin a field evaluation and report back to the school districts its findings. It was intended to prevent the Park Avenue experience from occurring again.

Before purchasing the property, in late April 1990, the Division of Oil and Gas conducted a Phase I environmental site investigation of the 11-acre site. It was damning.

"Location of the site was within the Los Angeles oilfield, and documented oil extraction on the site indicate a potential for environmental problems associated with explosive/toxic gases and subsurface soils contamination" … "Improperly abandoned oil wells are a recognized hazard due to their potential to act as a conduit for gas migration." … "Existing records may or may not correctly define the location and numbers of abandoned wells. The site could also contain such oilfield-related features as waste oil/drilling fluid sumps, buried pipelines, and other debris".

The inspection also identified several other environmental concerns.

On May 2, 1990, LAUSD General Counsel Richard Mason sent the bad news via fax to Mr. Cartwright. He informed Mr. Cartwright of the significant issues, identifying nine specific problems:

> "13 abandoned wells, probably more". "Alternative site, 1st & Beaudry – One well found; Manley believes other wells exist that could not be found; but less in number" …. Uncertainty – No one knows the

old practices of the drillers; shallow gas problem (unrelated to oil reservoir); a large concentration of concrete pavement may cause pressure to build up"..." Note: Approximately 2/3 of the site is free of known wells (2) Venting helps minimize gas problems, (3) This is the most troublesome, potentially problematic field in the entire LA basin, (4) DOG says this is a bad area for siting a school.... (6) This was an old industrial area – possibly toxics, (7) DOG's final line is that no structure should be built over well (This is a policy statement), (8) Central City West Plan has completely ignored this problem – not even mentioned, (9) Even the replacement housing site is on the edge of the field."

As a follow on, on May 8, 1990, R.K. Baker of the Division of Oil and Gas made the following observations:

[The Los Angeles] oil field is the most troublesome and problematic oil field in the entire county...

Anthony Patchett was the lead investigator on the Los Angeles County District Attorney's Belmont Task Force. He summarized the situation in an interview with Leslie Dutton on the Full Disclosure Network:

DUTTON: …is it possible that people wanted to get rid of that property and sell it to the Unified School District so they wouldn't have to clean it up?

PATCHETT: That's correct. In fact, the ironic thing is that when that property was appraised, that property was appraised as if there was no environmental contamination on the site. The State Division of Oil and Gas, in a letter written to LAUSD, told them they could not find a worse site imaginable to build a school.

And so Bonnie James from LAUSD sent the Division of Oil and Gas's severe concerns with the eleven-acre site to Shimizu and requested guidance. Dan Neimann of Shimizu arranged for a report to calm School Board member's fears. Mr. Niemann commissioned the predecessors of Law/Leroy Crandall and Associates to persuade the School Board that the Temple-Beaudry site could be used for a school site. The Leroy Crandall report says, in part:

"At present, the 780-acre Los Angeles City (oil) field that underlies the site is not included in a designated City of Los Angeles Methane District. The oil field has coexisted with residential and commercial surface uses for more than 90 years without significant problems. Any methane gas that might be released from the oil reservoir apparently dissipates into the atmosphere. Should methane gas be considered a future potential concern, installation of a methane barrier and venting system beneath the buildings at the time of construction would completely resolve the problem."

The report had a sunny conclusion:

"[I]n conclusion, the presence of oil wells is not a significantly unusual condition and is certainly not unique to the extent that it should result in project cancellation."

It was noted in our Belmont investigation that Leroy Crandall was a consultant for a Shimizu and had financial interests in having the 11-acre property used for a school, so it was financially important to him that the Shimizu Project in total would not be condemned.

Mr. Crandall minimized the problem and its solution:

"Should methane gas be considered a potential future concern, installation of a methane barrier and venting system beneath buildings at the time of construction would completely resolve the problem."

His company estimated the mitigation costs to be between $400,000 and $500,000.

LAUSD was pleased to hear this. Plans to build on the 11-acre junior high school site were to continue. Even the State Allocation

Board was alarmed. They referred to the site as the "Exxon Valdez" property.

But there were some people within the school district who were paying attention. Bonnie James wrote to Superintendent William Anton summarizing a June 14, 1990, Augmented Building Committee Meeting. She identified the preferred site as the First Street and Beaudry Avenue (24-acre site), not the Temple/Beaudry 11-acre site. She stated that Mr. Baker recommended that playing fields  be located over the abandoned wells to allow the natural venting of methane gas, that a gas venting and monitoring system be placed over the wells and under any structures, and that structures be located on the eastern portion of the site where there are no known wells. In December, the School Board began an initial study of the 24-acre site.

On September 30, 1992, Mr. Doug Brown, LAUSD's Building Division chief, wrote to school district staff saying that, in the context of using the total 35-acres for a high school site:

> "If we were to use this property for athletic fields,
> it would not be necessary to have a $2.5 million vapor
> barrier installed on the site."

According to Mr. Brown, the State Department of Education clearly indicated that if no buildings were placed on the site, the mitigation of methane within the zone was not necessary. As you can see, the problems were beginning to solve themselves.

Besides, Mr. Cartwright rationalized the situation in his interview with the Full Disclosure Network. According to him, people who live and work in downtown Los Angeles are already exposed to some amount of methane or hydrogen sulfide. What was a slight chance of exposure to some organic gases when compared to the dangers of riding busses on the Los Angeles freeways?

> "Well, we knew the oil field was there. A lot of the testing that was going on over time continued to reveal exactly the dimensions of the oil field. It's an old oil field. It's the Los Angeles oil field, one of the largest oil fields in the city. It's a shallow field, and it includes areas from Chinatown to the Ambassador Hotel at Western and Wilshire. So, it's quite an extensive field, and it's been largely tapped out. There's not much commercial production left. So, the learning process at the time was interesting, 'cause I actually had been an oil and gas lawyer in the '80s, so this was not something I didn't understand. And the first thing you do when you find out you're in an oil field is, you go and talk to the State Division of Oil and Gas, which is the leading State agency with knowledge of the field, and you start talking to the engineers and the State engineers, and my role is to make the school board understand the dimensions of the problem. And is it a serious problem? Everything's relative. After all, we're talking about a situation where 10,000 kids were getting bussed to the Valley, which is, itself, a problem, and a serious risk to students. So, you have to balance that against the condition of school sites in L.A. and what you can get."

So, what's wrong with a little toxic contamination on a school site? On October 31, 1999, Mr. Robert Bonner wrote an op-ed piece in the Los Angeles Times regarding the oil field hazards and mitigations related to the Belmont site. Mr. Bonner was a former U.S. Attorney and federal judge and was, at the time he wrote the article, a partner in the law firm of Gibson, Dunn & Crutcher. This law firm represented O'Melveny & Myers in a lawsuit initiated by the School District in connection with the Belmont project.

Mr. Bonner wrote that "[G]iven the prevalence of oil-field gases in the basin, well-tested and widely accepted technologies exist to protect against the potential dangers posed by their presence. For example, protection systems have been installed at hundreds of locations in Los Angeles, including the new downtown Central Library and the Page Museum on Wilshire Boulevard."

The "mitigation as needed" strategy used at Belmont was a formula for failure. When the school was eventually completed and opened in September 2008, it contained a gas mitigation system. The system included a methane barrier accompanied with a methane exhaust system underneath portions of the project to provide a double barrier of protection from methane gases. This gas mitigation system cost more than $17 million to design and install and will cost $250,000 to $500,000 a year to operate for the life of the school.

The buildings – where gases could potentially accumulate in dangerous concentrations – are protected by a plastic liner below the concrete slab. And below the liner are tubes to collect gas and carry it outside. Sensors that detect gas will trigger blowers to force it out more quickly. Backup blowers are available if needed. The entire system links to a touch-screen computer in the main office that has a live view of senor readings, which are recorded in a database.

So, the question is, why didn't the School District and its consultants and contractors include a mitigation system as part of the buildings when they began initial construction in 1997?

CHAPTER 9

How Dangerous is "Toxic"?

Methane and hydrogen sulfide gasses are present in the Los Angeles City Oil Field as they are in all oil fields. Methane is a colorless, odorless, and lighter-than-air gas that has the potential to create an explosion hazard, especially when confined in an enclosed space.

GeoChemical was a subcontractor of ABB Environmental. They conducted an investigation of "Near Surface Hydrocarbon Gas Accumulations" in soil on a property located between Boylston Street and Beaudry. Their report, prepared by GeoScience Analytical, Fleet E. Rust stated:

> "Since methane is present in concentrations at least four times the lower explosive limit, mitigation will be required if the construction of a school is undertaken."

At least four times the lower explosive limit. Most people would agree that is a dangerous amount of methane. And there was a history of this danger.

Late in the afternoon of March 24, 1985, methane gas that had been accumulating ignited in an auxiliary room of the Ross Dress-For-Less Department Store located on Third Street, in the Wilshire-Fairfax District of Los Angeles. The resulting explosion blew out the windows and partially collapsed the roof of the structure, reduced the store interior to a heap of twisted metal, and resulted in injuries requiring hospital treatment of 23 people.

Hydrogen sulfide is a colorless, heavier-than-air gas that has a rather distinct odor, similar to the smell of a rotten egg. Hydrogen sulfide is a very pernicious gas that Dr. Kaye Kilburn described to Leslie Dutton of the Full Disclosure Network:

DR. KILBURN: Well, besides being an awfully foul odor, it insidiously robs the brain of capacity to think, to remember, to do the ordinary cognitive functions – concentrate, co-process – but even things like balance, reaction time,  that we think of as very kind of primitive things that, you know, primates have had, and birds, for millions of years, are diminished or wiped out.

> DUTTON: Does it take much exposure for this to happen?
>
> DR. KILBURN: One or two, uh, breaths in the minimal exposure, if the concentration is right, the gas goes through the lung directly to the brain. It has no chance to be detoxified.

Later onsite measurements of the property located between Boylston Street and Beaudry identified the quantity of hydrogen sulfide.

When Joe Walton reported hydrogen sulfide odors during excavation, LAUSD's Richards Lui scrambled to the site to verify the quantities. Gary Dorn of Law/Crandall claimed he was getting readings of 200 ppm (parts per million) of hydrogen sulfide. Employees of Foster/Wheeler Environmental were also present and indicated they had readings of 1,000 ppm of organic vapors. Apparently, when Mr. Lui arrived, the hydrogen sulfide went into hiding. Readings taken by Mr. Dorn in Mr. Lui's presence showed 0 ppm.

Dr. Kilburn put a logical point to the differences:

> "I think they're not trusting their nose, is what it comes down to. The site smells. It smells of hydrogen sulfide. The human nose can detect 30 parts per billion. It's now been recommended from the U.S. Government that one part per billion is the toxic level to avoid. Levels of 375 parts per million – that, I think, is 375,000 parts per billion – have been found at the Belmont site after rains, where there are puddles where gas can be collected by simply inverting a jar and letting the gas bubble in."

One part per BILLION is the toxic level to avoid. In other words, if ycan smell it, it's dangerous.

In his interview, Ed Scott explained how the Government views hydrogen sulfide:

> SCOTT: Well, first off, the State presumes that it is a hazardous toxic waste. The Federal government says that it is, and I can read to you from the Agency for Toxic Substances and Disease Registry. Hydrogen

sulfide is considered a broad-spectrum poison, meaning it can poison several different systems in the body. Breathing very high levels of hydrogen sulfide can cause death within a few breaths. There could be loss of consciousness after one or more breaths.

DUTTON: So, in your estimation, if the school is built and it still has the presence of hydrogen sulfide, is that a violation of State law?

SCOTT: Yes. It's a violation of State and Federal law.

DUTTON: Now, is it dangerous to children?

SCOTT: It's extremely dangerous to children, and one of the reasons that it is is that it tends to hang low towards the ground, and children being shorter in stature are more likely to breathe in fumes from it.

Dr. Kilburn thinks putting children in this kind of exposure is criminal.

"Some of you will remember the 1992 earthquake at Long Beach and Wilmington. That turned out not to be an earthquake at all, but it was an explosion of the desulphurization plant at Texaco down north of Pacific Coast Highway. Twenty thousand people, at least, were exposed to hydrogen sulfide. What does it do to children Well, from two schools, special education teachers came to me for their own problems, and then said, 'I have students who were passing and can't pass anymore. I have had more referrals for special education since that explosion than I ever remember having, and I have seen many children drop out of school because they're uneducable.' If this is what we want as a Belmont High School, we already have seen, at Wilmington School, how this plays out. I don't really think it can be justified to do the experiment again. It was conclusive the first time."

CHAPTER 10

Let's Make a Deal

Public officials wanted affordable housing in the Belmont area of Los Angeles. Because Shimizu and LAUSD were afraid of publicity, face-to-face meetings were held at the Checkers Hotel in downtown Los Angeles. In June 1993, Shimizu's outside counsel, Timi Hallem of Tuttle and Taylor, met with David Cartwright (LAUSD's outside counsel) and LAUSD General Counsel Richard Mason. Mr. Cartwright also invited Dominic Shambra to the meeting.

Mr. Shambra was the first and only Director of LAUSD's Office of Planning and Development, which was established by the School Board in the 1993-1994 school year. This office was unique in that it reported directly to the Superintendent's office – outside the normal division and branch reporting relationships. From our research, it became apparent that Mr. Shambra was the lead management representative of LAUSD regarding the Belmont project, especially for the site acquisition and funding phases. This seemed to be a  significant responsibility for an employee whose previous responsibilities included serving as a playground supervisor.

Mr. Cartwright had previously worked with Mr. Shambra on the Grand Avenue parking garage joint venture. This joint venture was a unique combination of a private company using or leasing the school property and then paying a fee to the school district. Mr. Shambra was considering building and utilizing the Belmont project with the same concept. LAUSD was fascinated with the idea of making money from school property. Thus, Mr. Shambra was charged with proceeding full steam ahead with the full authority of the Superintendent.

Although LAUSD preferred the land near First Street and Beaudry Avenue, under Mr. Cartwright's stewardship, the school district settled in their negotiation for a $30 million price tag for not only the northern 11 acres but the entire 24-acre parcel. Environmental problems? No problem. Everybody seemed to ignore or at least minimize the known hazards on the site. In his defense, Mr. Cartwright later declared his role as legal counsel was limited in nature and scope and did not involve legal advice on environmental matters. Mr. Cartwright merely reported to Mr. Mason. Besides, the school district had been building on contaminated property for decades. The next problem: where was Mr. Shambra going to get $30 million?

Another site LAUSD was considering was the Ambassador Hotel (owned by Donald Trump) in downtown Los Angeles. It had been sitting dormant for years since the assassination of Robert Kennedy. So, the school district had been threatening to flex its muscle and use its power of eminent domain to condemn the site. In fact, LAUSD had a previous allocation from the State Allocation Board, under the California Department of Education that was intended for the condemnation of the Ambassador Hotel site.

Shambra bullied the State Allocation Board to get them to agree to shift $25 million from other LAUSD projects. The school district had allocated air conditioning for the schools slated for multi-track scheduling (school continuing through summer). Shambra reasoned that since the Belmont project would alleviate the overcrowding problem, the multi-track schedule would not need to be implemented. Therefore, the air conditioning money could be allocated to the Belmont property purchase.

Mr. Shambra was an effective salesman. On September 22, 1993, the State Allocation Board relented to Mr. Shambra's pressure and approved LAUSD's request to transfer $30 million from air conditioning projects to purchase the 11-acre parcel at the north end of the property.

But that was the toxic end of the field. It would cost a fortune to mitigate the contamination of the old oil field on the north 11 acres. To resolve the mitigation expense, Shambra needed to purchase the whole 35-acre parcel and use the north end for the athletic fields.

Mr. Shambra and General Counsel Mason leaned on the State Allocation Board once again with their hard-sell tactics. Mr. Mason and Mr. Shambra demanded that Senator Greene and the Allocation Board transfer money currently allocated for the Ambassador Hotel site and set the money aside for the purchase of the additional twenty-acre Shimizu site. Mr. Mason pitched it hard, advising them that "what is before them is an opportunity that, if not taken today, will be lost." He claimed that "the landowners (Shimizu) cannot say that the opportunity will be available next month, so he believes that the golden opportunity could be lost if the Board doesn't approve the project today."

California State Assembly Member Peace wasn't convinced. He knew the school district hadn't adequately vetted the site. He didn't respond well to their hard sale pitch:

"… It was indicated to us that this site was – was ready to be acquired and, indeed, if it weren't acquired now, it would not likely be ready as of the first of the year, and now you're telling me there is no EIR [Environmental Impact Review]. There is no appraisal? What is there?"

Mr. Mason responded, "I think we have an offer to sell – to buy that particular property…"

Assembly Member Peace jumped on him, noting that no appraisal was done. Mr. Mason lamely responded, "Contingent on the EIR, we know what the appraisal would be. We don't have it officially. It's being accomplished at this point."

Peace was beside himself. "Do you think this Board is going to sit here and let you dip into that $50 million, and if Trump thinks this Board is going to sit here and let you dip into the $50 million, then you're both nuts. We're going to fight that tooth and nail. It's your responsibility and not the taxpayers!"

Undaunted, Mr. Mason went back to the LAUSD School Board and confronted them with a new idea. He suggests that in response to the EIR requirement of the State Allocation Board, his staff would present the State Board with a negative declaration, not a full EIR.

Instead of an EIR, a Mitigated Negative Declaration is a Negative Declaration prepared for a project when the initial study has identified potentially significant effects on the environment, but the effects after the mitigation would no longer pose a significant risk to the environment because the project was revised. The revisions to the project plans must mitigate the harmful effects on the environment, and there must be no substantial evidence that the revised project will negatively affect the environment.

Mr. Mason had convinced himself that grading and moving fill around on land covered with old oil wells, seeping with oil, smelling of methane and hydrogen sulfide would "not have a significant impact on the environment."

Mr. Mason claimed the negative declaration is "legally defensible in this case since the site has been studied already," regarding the northern 11-acres. He stated that he anticipated legal challenges but wasn't concerned. "The Shimizu owners are aware of the situation and would agree to still pursue the sale if challenges are made."

On the Full Disclosure Network, oil and gas expert Ed Scott explained what Mason was trying to do with this "negative declaration." He told host Leslie Dutton:

> "Well, it was a declaration prepared by, I assume, the school district, that – where they decided that it was an acceptable site to build on. Generally, you wouldn't do that on a school site. The proper thing would have been to have done a Phase I. I mean, to me, the catch point in this whole thing was: When they got the very first Phase I and said, "This is an oil field site. There's a potential for earthquake faults on this site. You should slow down, stop, and look." That should have been the first trigger to say, "This is not a good site for us."

"But instead, they moved on, and they moved on from that consultant to another consultant, and they moved from consultant to consultant to consultant, until they finally got the one that they wanted, which said, "There's no problem where you have the buildings.""

With their usual hard-nosed diplomacy, Mr. Mason and Mr. Shambra pressured the LAUSD School Board, ultimately convincing the Board that all was well. They convinced LAUSD to release "Findings of Fact" for the 24-acre site, approving and justifying the Mitigated Negative Declaration. The School Board stated in this document that they had satisfied the CEQA requirements.

The California Environmental Quality Act (CEQA) was passed by the California legislature in 1970, shortly after the U.S. federal  government passed the National Environmental Policy Act. The California legislation was to institute a statewide policy of environmental protection. CEQA does not directly regulate land uses but instead requires state and local agencies within California to follow a protocol of analysis and public disclosure of the potential environmental impacts of development projects.

Since the School Board stated they had satisfied the CEQA requirements, the bewildered State Allocation Board had no choice but to relent.

The Purchase and Sale Agreement was executed on December 17, 1993. Under the contract negotiated by Mr. Cartwright, the District agreed to purchase the property "as is" and without warranty for environmental conditions. Section nine of the agreement reads:

> "Buyer acknowledges that it has been informed of
> the environmental issues set forth on Exhibit E hereto,
> including without limitation, the fact that there are oil
> wells on a portion of the property, and that a portion
> of the property was previously used as a gas station."

Some people later speculated that the "as is" phrase was meant to assure that Shimizu would never be blamed for the environmental hazards on the property and would never be required to mitigate or clean up the site. Roger Carrick served on the Los Angeles County District Attorney's Special Belmont Task Force, which was charged with investigating the Belmont Learning Complex disaster for possible criminal prosecution. Mr. Carrick suggested another reason the School Board settled on buying the property "as is."

> "As I understand it from our investigation, the
> decision was made because they thought they were

> getting a good price. If you recall, real estate prices plummeted in the mid-'90s. People had paid a lot of money for this property in the late '80s, and it was being sold at a significant discount."
>
> "We can all debate whether they got the right number for it, but I think that was their logic. If the seller was willing to sell it at that price, they would

buy it. And you can imagine a school district has a very hard time finding large – this was a very big piece of property. Sixty acres in downtown Los Angeles is impossible to come by. So, this was a very hard decision the school district had to make. They needed to build a new high school, and they decided to buy it 'as is,' I'm sure to preserve their price."

Later, Mr. Cartwright explained that it was just a standard boilerplate for the purchase of any property.

"The 25-acre piece of the Belmont project that was acquired with that "as is" phrase included a whole series of reps and warranties on the site itself, and then the final phrase, "except as promised in this agreement, site is as-is." That site is not the oil field problem site. It's the adjacent 10 acres that had been bought by the District in the mid-'80s. That 25-acre site was a substantially clean site. It had primarily been a residential site, and the oil field only impacts that site at the margins. 'As is,' by the way, is a customary commercial term, and in purchase contracts for commercial real estate, it probably appears in about 90% of commercial contracts in Los Angeles."

He was also adamant that if LAUSD had seized the property utilizing its power of eminent domain, that it would have been acquired "as is" anyway.

What did LAUSD purchase when they settled on the property "as is"? This is troubling beyond comprehension.

CHAPTER 11

The Environmental Assessment Sham

There were procedures and controls established to prevent disasters like Belmont. The State of California mandated that school districts had to assure they were building safe and fiscally responsible schools. These included specific points of evaluation that would have given LAUSD the opportunity to foresee the tremendous liability and stop the process before it became the nightmare that eventually occurred. What caused the failure of these systems with Belmont? Systems are only as good as the people who follow them and enforce them.

It started with the way the LAUSD handled the Phase I and Phase II environmental studies.

In the jargon of real estate, due diligence requirements are standard and accepted real estate practices that are part of buying and selling a property. These investigations include ordering a preliminary title report for the property and examining the title for any easements (that is, use restrictions) on the property that might adversely affect the proposed school use; investigating any potentially costly onsite requirements such as grading hilly areas and/or offsite requirements to develop the property into a school facility such as road widening, sidewalks, etc..

Most importantly, in the context of siting schools on potentially contaminated lands, due diligence requirements set out what sort of environmental investigation is needed to determine if a site is polluted from past uses. This preliminary environmental site assessment generally is called a Phase I site assessment.

To satisfy due diligence requirements, a comprehensive Phase I assessment will reference and interpret a variety of sources of information, including:

- a title search to identify previous owners and users;
- aerial photographs dating as far back in time as possible to ascertain prior uses of the property;
- regulatory lists, both state and federal, to identify reported leaking underground storage tanks, generators of hazardous waste, and releases of harmful substances, both onsite and offsite within a one-half to one-mile radius;
- information on site geology to assess the potential for migration of contaminants, potential impacts to groundwater, etc.;
- regulatory agency files to determine current conditions and pending enforcement actions;
- a site visit to discover signs of potentially hazardous conditions, discolored soils or paving, leaking drums, standing water;
- interviews with owners and employees to understand the nature of the business being conducted on the premises; and
- a review of operating plans, hazardous materials, or waste handling programs also may be appropriate.

A Phase I typically is conducted by an environmental consultant, and its objective is to identify potential environmental liabilities associated with the property. If the initial site assessment does not rule out the possibility of contamination, a more detailed site assessment, a Phase II, typically is required, which includes site sampling and an initial risk assessment.

After the environmental assessment and other due diligence investigations are completed, the school district staff typically will hold a second round of community meetings to review the information and answer questions about the preferred site. If the community does not mount strong political opposition to the site at this time, the school board typically will approve the site for a new school.

Back on May 22, 1989, as part of the Shimizu Pacific Basin Center, ABB Environmental had begun the CEQA process and conducted a Phase I assessment of the Belmont site. They documented the presence of hydrocarbons, noting problems with groundwater and, of course, the abandoned oil wells.

Not to be dissuaded by such a bleak report, Robert Niccum, working for LAUSD as the Director of Real Estate, pushed the project forward. Mr. Niccum, designated by the School District as a "CEQA officer"—wrote a letter dated July 22, 1993, to LAUSD's General Counsel Richard Mason advocating the negative declaration concept. Mr. Cartwright, serving as the lead attorney for LAUSD on the project, jumped on the idea and advised that the School District use the prior CEQA work to shorten the time for the CEQA process.

Having short-circuited the Phase I, the state agencies wanted to assure that a proper Phase II would be conducted. On January 18, 1994, Henry Heydt, the Assistant Director or the California Department of Education's School Facilities Planning Division, wrote a letter to the LAUSD School Board to express his serious concerns.

Mr. Heydt emphatically stated that "approval is contingent upon the Phase II environmental assessment results that would ensure the health and safety of the students and would be consistent with the cost standards of the Office of Local Assistance." In other words, the

Phase II had to demonstrate that any hazards could be rendered safe at a reasonable cost.

On February 15, 1994, Susie Wong, the Director of LAUSD's Environmental Health & Safety branch, prepared a Request for Proposal to select "a qualified firm to provide Phase II environmental assessment services for Belmont New Senior High School."

Two days later, with the RFP in the works, General Counsel Richard Mason informed the LAUSD School Board that the State Allocation Board was taking up the issue of "allocation of funds to acquire the Shimizu property." In this memorandum, Mr. Mason described the demands by the State Allocation Board regarding abandoning the Ambassador site and complying with all environmental reviews. In a stunning display of make-believe, he then told the School Board, **"we have met all conditions."**

The folks in Sacramento weren't as easily misled as the LAUSD School Board. Later that month, the State Allocation Board strongly reiterated its demand that LAUSD still needed to complete a Phase II site assessment of the property. For some reason, this surprised Mr. Cartwright, and a meeting was called.

To expedite this irritating obstacle, David Cartwright, Richard Mason, David Koch, Robert Niccum, and Dominic Shambra came up with the idea of by-passing the LAUSD's Environmental Health & Safety Branch, who said the study would take several months. Impatient with the Branch's formalized process and deliberate pace. Mr. Cartwright and Mr. Shambra decided to pressure Shimizu to conduct the Phase II study.

Under the gun, Shimizu contracted with ENV America to conduct a "down-dated" Phase II study of the site. Under pressure from Mr. Cartwright, Shimizu utilized a 1989 McLaren Report as a baseline of information on the site. Between February 19 and February 22,

1994, ENV America merely confirmed the old report by taking soil boring samples to confirm the results of the previous investigation. Their report was submitted in the first week of March.

There was a loud cry of "Sham!" coming from people who knew that a thorough Phase II could not have been completed in 48 hours. Caught between a rock and a hard place, Mr. Niccum had to admit the "ENV America study fell far short of examining and reporting on matters which the District would have required of a consultant." He noted that the contrived Phase II neglected to quantify "hazardous substances and waste sources" and "quantify contaminants, determine the degree of contamination and extent of offsite migration." Basically, everything important to the safety of the school and the surrounding community.

The in-fighting began. Mr. Koch criticized Mr. Shambra for excluding LAUSD's Environmental Health & Safety Branch. Superintendent Sidney Thompson came to the defense of Mr. Shambra and asserted his authority to make sure that the Environmental Health & Safety Branch would be effectively excluded from any further work on Belmont.

But then, nothing happened. Following the closing of the sale on March 15, 1994, no one continued to investigate the contamination of the site. A lot of people threw rocks at each other during the fracas, but once the ink was dry, nobody seemed to care anymore.

As Ed Scott said in his interview with the Full Disclosure Network:

> "Well, they got a lot of advice, and they got a
> lot of reports. If they didn't like the report, as I said
> previously, it appeared to me that they found somebody

that would write them the report that they wanted. Sometimes they just overlooked it and ignored it..."

Regarding the exclusion of LAUSD's Environmental Health & Safety Branch, he said:

"Most school districts have a person within their organization that has some environmental knowledge that would say that this site would have triggered and they would say, 'This is potentially a problem site.' It's in an earthquake zone, we know it is, there's a fault there, number one. Number two, it's in oil fields that have been there for many, many years, and it poses a risk. Not only posed a risk to the kids that were going to be at that school, but it has posed a risk to the neighborhood, too..."

His concern about the neighborhood required additional commentary.

"One of the issues that came up in the neighborhood was that there were higher levels of methane coming into homes around the site and that methane alarms were going off during the construction of it. The school district said, 'Well, it's not our fault. We have nothing to do with it.' But the reality is, they were changing the soil conditions of the property. That property had been loosely compacted, native, natural, and those methane gasses were being allowed to come up through the soil and dissipate into the air. Once they started moving soil around and compacting it, it essentially put a cap on the property, and that methane started moving horizontally, and it moved into the neighborhoods..."

Belmont was going to be a hazard for the work crews trying to build the school, the kids trying to attend the school, and even the neighbors, trying to live in the homes around the school.

CHAPTER 12

Show Me the Money

The LAUSD Office of Planning & Development went to work. Encouraged by Dominic Shambra, the LAUSD Facilities and Operations Committee approved the establishment of the Belmont Learning Complex. They authorized proceeding with Request for Proposal for the Temple Beaudry Public-Private Joint Venture.

The District had three realistic options to fund the Belmont Learning Complex:

1. They could rob funds from the Proposition BB bond approved by voters
2. They could seek reimbursement of construction costs from the State Allocation Board
3. They could use general fund money or appropriate tax-exempt borrowing through Certificates of Participation.

They did all three.

Shambra first leaned on the Proposition BB Oversight Committee. They caved in and agreed to consider reimbursing LAUSD for up to 50% of the Belmont construction cost *IF* Shambra could get the California State Allocation Board to spring for the initial 50%.

Director Shambra created a first working budget for the Belmont project to solicit the 50% from the State Allocation Board. This application was submitted on February 26, 1997, with primary assistance from an outside consultant Dr. Betty Hanson, who had previously worked with the California Department of Education.

In Ms. Hanson's previous job, Ms. Hanson began approving schools with unsettled toxic issues, as far back as 1989. She signed the final approval letter for construction on the contaminated school site that became the problematic Jefferson Middle School in Los Angeles, along with eight other LAUSD school sites where toxic concerns were known at the time of approval. Betty Hanson left the employ of the California Department of Education in 1994 and was hired two months later by Mr. Shambra to work for LAUSD at $125.00 per hour as a consultant. Mr. Shambra knew an ally when he saw one.

This application submitted to the State Allocation Board identified Belmont as a "design/build" project. In this process, the developer/contractor would guarantee completed construction for a "Guaranteed Maximum Price." In correspondence from Matthew Witte, Mr. Witte attempted to "refine the development budget with the goal of producing a target Guaranteed Maximum Price. In his letter, Mr. Witte stated, "The 'High School Budget' has often been referred to as a 'not to exceed a number of $65 million'."

The price identified in Shambra's Disposition and Development Agreement was almost $86 million. But the totals in the application submitted to the School Allocation Board came out to over $93 million, significantly above the Guaranteed Maximum Price in the agreement. It was apparent that Mr. Shambra contemplated seeking reimbursement for costs far and above the basic school portion of Belmont.

A lurking problem was the potential cost of the environmental cleanup and remediation. As stipulated in the Disposition and Development Agreement, the Guaranteed Maximum Price could be increased, resulting in an unlimited cost ceiling if any of the following expenses were incurred:

- For hazardous material remediation
- For cost associated with CEQA (California Environmental Quality Act) requirements
- For changes in the school components
- For costs involving site conditions (oil field conditions and hazardous materials)
- For delays in construction caused by site conditions

In the Disposition and Development Agreement, Temple Beaudry Partners was "exculpated" from these costs or delays. Apparently, someone on their staff knew what was coming. But Mr. Shambra and Dr. Hanson were not deterred by the unmitigated disaster they were facilitating, even though they were fully aware of the situation.

Astoundingly, there was no request for reimbursement for any remediation of the environmental cost associated with Belmont. Mr. Shambra and Dr. Hanson consciously made a "judgment call" not to include any estimate of the environmental cleanup or remediation in their budgets. In later interviews, Mr. Shambra defended this decision, claiming that these costs were uncertain and that the State Allocation Board would not reimburse "contingent" costs, and including them was "not a smart political move to make" and in fact might have jeopardized the entire application.

The fact that Mr. Shambra and Dr. Hanson failed to prepare a reasonable evaluation and contingency budget to accommodate the significant environmental hazards existing in the land under the Belmont project effectively blinded LAUSD from making a realistic appraisal of the likely environmental costs that would ultimately be incorporated into the completion of the Belmont Learning Complex. This failure became the tripwire that would eventually bring down the entire project.

Later in 1997, the State Allocation Board denied Mr. Shambra's application, forcing him to find other means of funding.

In Shambra's mind, these state regulations against building on a contaminated site, the obstructive bond committees, and the restrictive requirements from state boards weren't obligations and rules to be followed. Even though they were instituted to protect the school districts, the public taxpayers, and future students — to him, they were unnecessary impediments.

They were merely temporary barriers that needed to be "knocked down," as David Cartwright claimed in an interview with the Full Disclosure Network. They were obstacles to be run over. Shambra wasn't about to let a bunch of silly bureaucrats stop him.

CHAPTER 13

The "Secret" Funds

It costs a lot of money to build a school, especially when all the land is gone, and in-fill is the only opportunity for new construction. For almost 34 years, LAUSD hadn't built a new school. And the existing schools were lacking modern equipment and deteriorating rapidly. LAUSD was cornered by the 1978 passage of California's historic Proposition 13, the renowned People's Initiative to Limit Property Taxation. Proposition 13 restricted government agencies from increasing property taxes without a problematic two-thirds majority vote of the public. There was no money to build new schools.

The voters had turned down several bond issues. In 1994, the electorate refused both 1B: Safe Schools Act and 1C: Higher Education Facilities Bond Act. People simply weren't interested in paying higher taxes. California Assembly Speaker Bob Hertzberg finally mounted a massively funded statewide publicity campaign and eventually – in March 1995 – got the electorate to approve Proposition 203: The Public Education Facilities Bond Act. This vote authorized the state to sell $3 billion in general obligation bonds for K-12 schools and higher education facilities.

Proposition 203 was a watershed vote. LAUSD quickly mounted its own local ballot issue. Proposition BB was a massive school bond measure that authorized the school district to sell $2.4 billion in bonds for the construction of new schools and the repair and modernization of existing schools throughout the District. Additionally, it was to improve local schools and relieve classroom overcrowding. The ballot measure was approved in April 1997 by 71% of voters. In a controversial decision, in June 1997, the Proposition BB Oversight Committee agreed that it would use Proposition BB funds to reimburse the school district up to 50% of Belmont's construction cost, contingent upon the school district securing the initial 50% from the California State Allocation Board. The tap was now open and flowing. And the developers and contractors began circling.

The California Legislature continued to chum the waters. Proposition 1A, the Kindergarten-University Public Education Facilities Bond Act of 1998, was approved by the voters the following November 1998. This Proposition provided $6.7 billion in general obligation bonds for K–12 public school facilities and produced the first funding for the new School Facility Program. The School Facility Program provided California State funding assistance for two major types of facilities construction projects: new construction and modernization. At the time of the passage of this proposition it was the largest school bond in the history of California.

Dominic Shambra saw all this money swirling around him, but there was none for him. The State Allocation Board had denied Shambra's application, which in turn dried up the funds contingently promised by the Proposition BB Oversight Committee. Then Shambra talked to Wayne Wedin.

The relationship between Wayne Wedin and Dominic Shambra was a match made in Heaven (or Hell, depending). Wedin was known to have horse-traded a contaminated site for a developer and then helped the Brea-Olinda School District build a school on that property. In his book "The Road to Belmont," Bryan Steele noted that Wedin:

"While a member of the Brea City Council, he successfully pushed through a $320,000 public works contract involving a firm that was paying him $41,000 on another project. That contract was later canceled, and in 1992, Wedin was tried and acquitted of criminal conflict of interest charges."

He was undoubtedly a wheeler-dealer that impressed Shambra. Wedin introduced Shambra to the concept of "joint-venture" or "joint-use" as a means of developing land whereby two distinct entities jointly combine their resources so that both can benefit from the project. For example, schools will combine with communities to support and utilize swimming pools and athletic fields. The problem was it wasn't legal in California for schools to combine with commercial entities.

In his interview with the Full Disclosure Network, Scott Wildman, who was serving in the California State Legislature as Chairman of the Joint Legislative Audit Committee noted:

"When the Belmont project was kicking into high gear in '94, the LAUSD put forward legislation which would allow for design/builds, for the kind of project that this is, which wasn't allowed in State law. That legislation, unfortunately, didn't pass. Yet the school district still proceeded with that process, and so we didn't have, on the State level, any real oversight or any real ability to stop a project."

Shambra and Wedin went steamrolling full speed ahead. They convinced the beleaguered School Board that they could actually get commercial entities to fund the building project. While the school district sent its lobbyists up to Sacramento to pass AB482 to permit such co-mingling of school district and private funds, Shambra and his Office of Planning & Development were out recruiting. There were plans for a Ralph's grocery store and pharmacy. Payless Shoes and McDonald's offered to install retail outlets.

Local politicians were all excited when Shambra offered to provide low-cost housing within the Belmont Learning Complex. In a letter to School Board President Jeff Horton, then Los Angeles City Councilman Michael Hernandez stated:

> "The City has placed a high priority on rehabilitating our urban neighborhoods, and this project demonstrates this interest and concern. The combination of school, recreation/community services, retail, and housing is one of the best things that could happen to this community and the constituents we all serve."

The word "complex" indeed described the intensive real estate contracts that were being proposed, offered, and considered. All of them were far above Dominic Shambra's business acumen as a former playground supervisor. But Shambra was not about to be left alone – not when he had this massive budget at his personal direction. So-called experts were flocking to Shambra offering to solve all his problems, each of them justifying a substantial fee.

At the top of the heap was Wayne Wedin, who was enjoying a lucrative contract to guide Shambra. Since 1987, LAUSD had contracted with Mr. Wedin approximately 14 times, and almost always, the sponsor was Dominic Shambra. These contracts were substantial, totaling nearly $1 million. Many of these contracts featured unexplained "extensions" and "amendments."

In later investigations, documents relating to these contracts and payments were somehow missing. One example: an invoice sent to Shambra didn't specify critical information such as the dates and the work to be performed. Instead, the date was shown as "various." And the description of the work was "Overall research and contact with developer community." A total of 40 hours was billed in this fashion on this one invoice.

According to Shambra, things couldn't be better. He was in hog heaven. Listening to Wedin, Shambra was convinced that all of these business entities would pay for the building and maintenance of this massive Belmont Learning Complex. In their wildest dreams, Shambra and Wedin hinted that the school district could even make a profit in this speculative adventure. The School Board was seduced by this siren song.

In his interview with the Full Disclosure Network, Scott Wildman was disappointed by the enthusiasm of the school district towards this project:

> "Because that's their core mission, is to educate. To build schools and to educate. And the State's mission is to support them, is to find the money to make sure that we educate these kids, we buy them textbooks, and we actually build schools. The problem is, school districts or any government agency is not really in the business of making money. They shouldn't be in the business of making money, because there's a risk whenever you're in the business of making money.

You can't risk the future of our kids. The State of California needs to be the kind of entity that doesn't risk the future of these kids, that doesn't put millions of dollars into harebrained schemes and in the end, have nothing for those kids, no school for those kids to go to."

But Dominic Shambra's Wild Ride was just beginning. As stated earlier, Shambra reported directly to the Superintendent (at this time Bill Anton), rather than reporting up the chain-of-command through facilities. As Bryan Steele noted:

"Compounding this reporting irregularity was the decision of the Board of Education to funnel all short-term revenues generated by the OPD's joint-venture projects into a separate account exclusively controlled by Shambra. This method of reinvestment allowed Shambra to spend funds as he sought fit, including the hiring of outside consultants at exorbitant tees."

Shambra's next problem: how was he going to come up with the $91.4 million to get this school off the ground (literally!)? He was gently persuaded to utilize an insidious device that had been used by the school district for years to circumvent the restrictions of Proposition 13 – Certificates of Participation (COPs) became the source of funding for the Belmont Learning Complex.

"Many people think that they get to vote on every issuance of bonds in California, and I need to educate them that that's simply not true. There's a large proportion of debt sold in California, known as either lease bonds or lease revenue bonds or certificates of participation. For those of us in financial circles, those are known as COPS, and those are increasingly common."

This shocking statement came from Kathleen Connell, who from 1995 to 2003, was the California State Controller. She said this in an interview on the Full Disclosure Network. Shocking because, according to the voters who in 1978 passed California's notorious Proposition 13, the *people* get to vote to increase their taxes – according to the People's Initiative to Limit Property Taxation. This proposition decreased property taxes by assessing property values at

their 1975 value and restricted annual increases of the assessed value of real property to an inflation factor, not to exceed 2% per year. It also contained language requiring a nearly impossible two-thirds majority in both legislative houses for future increases of any state tax rates.

So how could municipalities, water districts, and especially school districts get money from the stingy and intractable public? They would offer COP's. As Ms. Connell said:

"Well, in order to avoid going to the people constantly for every little additional financing that a city, a county, a special district wanted to do, the lawyers devised a mechanism by which the state or the city or a municipal borough would say that they would issue a certificate of participation. What that does, without any vote of the legislature, or without any vote of the people, (emphasis added) it goes to the vote of the governing body and it says, 'We're going to use debt financing, borrowing money, to build a library downtown, for example, in Los Angeles.'

"In that situation, you have to concoct a scheme that there is an essential use of that building. The essential use was the library. You commit that library as collateral to the bondholder, that if you fail to make your payments in a timely  fashion, that they can then own that building – I don't know what they would do with the downtown central library, but they would be able to own that building as a way of getting their bond security."

She gave an extreme example from Oakland, California:

"Oakland was very creative, and they actually used, as collateral, the pipes that ran through the City of Oakland to deliver water to people. Well, obviously, they weren't going to default on paying for their certificate of participation because people wouldn't want their water supply shut off. What it does is allow them another stream of financing that many voters are blind to."

"What it also does is invoke a political privilege. They determine that a bond financing is not important enough, not visible enough, not broad enough, to bring to the voter and the voter's attention. Or they're making a political judgment, that if they brought it to the voter, the voter might say "No." And so, if they use the COP financing structure, then they avoid that involvement of the voter in the process."

In another interview on the Full Disclosure Network, Leslie Dutton asked former LAUSD School Board Member David Tokofsky about the use of COPs:

DUTTON: Why was it that BB bond money, the traditional general obligation bonds were not used with Belmont?

TOKOFSKY: Well, from the political consultants, there was a clear message from polls and otherwise that if you put Belmont on as general obligation bond, the bond would lose. And therefore, a different approach was recommended.

DUTTON: And the difference between a general obligation bond and a certificate of participation bond is what?

TOKOFSKY: Well, the general obligation bond, you go to the voters, and you had to get two-thirds of the voters of the jurisdiction in order to get the approval to do it. The certificates of participation are a tool that legally the elected representatives have the ability to publicly disclose that they're gonna issue these, have a debate, and then finance them out of the general fund rather than a separate fund. So, you issue, let's say, $300 million of COPs, you'll go to Wall Street to get that money, but the payment of the interest and principal comes out of the general fund. So, teachers' salaries, books, supplies are, in essence paying for the Board-issued certificate of participation.

Ms. Dutton pressed Mr. Tokofsky, drawing the revenue line back to the taxpayers:

DUTTON: When you say that teachers' salaries, coming out of the general fund, and that was paying for the COP bonds?

TOKOFSKY: Paying for the interest and the principal to pay back, yes.

DUTTON: Well, how -- where does the money for the teachers' salaries come from? General obligation bonds?

TOKOFSKY: No. The general fund comes from predominantly from property taxes through the State Capitol back to the local district.

DUTTON: So, in other words, COPs are paid for out of property taxes?

TOKOFSKY: They're paid for, uh -- let me see if I follow... Uh... Yeah -- I would -- uh, you probably could draw that line, that in essence the payback of the obligation of the certificate of participation coming  from the general fund, which is predominantly from the property taxes...

Then he quickly defended the need for using COP's:

TOKOFSKY: . . . Using Certificates of Participation is a legally accepted way in which local governments have approached the post Prop 13 era shortage of funds . . .

On December 9, 1997, the school district closed the sale of $91.4 million in Certificates of Participation. The debt was secured by many LAUSD properties but did not include Belmont itself. In this manner, the financing did not have to contend with the typical disclosures regarding the environmental conditions at Belmont. Then-LAUSD Chief Financial Officer Henry Jones knew what he was doing.

In May of 1998, Mr. Jones wrote a letter to Raymond Rodriguez, who was functioning *de facto* as a project officer for Belmont. He warned that the misuse of Certificates of Participation could jeopardize the tax-exempt status of the COPs.

Enter the Internal Revenue Service. Would this gorilla agency finally be the one entity to put a stop to the abusive and unchecked behavior of the LAUSD?

CHAPTER 14

LAUSD vs. the Internal Revenue Service

"You have to look hard to find a description inside there as to what really occurred because it's just like the investors that purchase the COPs. The environmental conditions were excluded from the property appraisal. There were conflicts of interest. The retail infrastructure was built with certificates of participation funds. There were fraudulent bills submitted to the LAUSD, and there was a question as to the actual tax status."

That's what Anthony Patchett told Leslie Dutton in an interview with the Full Disclosure Network. Mr. Patchett was a former Special Assistant Los Angeles District Attorney, who headed the Belmont Task Force. He was  intimately involved with the Belmont investigation. He also stated:

"The COPs that were used in Belmont was approximately $92 million were issued in COPs. And as I mentioned, between $12-25 million was used to build the retail infrastructure. And that's an illegal and criminal use."

The LAUSD was encouraged to use COPs as a funding source because they offered many attractive aspects:

1. They do not require voter approval. The school district knew the voters would never approve raising taxes to fund Belmont. COPs allowed them to circumvent the 2/3 voter approval requirement of Prop 13.
2. They are more attractive to bond buyers because they offer higher interest rates, and the IRS excluded from reporting the higher interest as income.

The problem was the joint-venture project.

Even though the laws governing school construction didn't allow it, Mr. Shambra was going ahead full-throttle on the retail portion of the school. In his interview with the Full Disclosure Network, he explained the progress this way:

> SHAMBRA: . . . But it [the school] was on top of a parking structure, which a part of it would be used for the school and part would be used if the District wanted to put offices in it, or if they wanted to use it for retail, or if they wanted to use it for other government activities, they could. But we had to build that podium in order to put the school on the same level. So, the certificates were for – if the retail had not taken place, which it didn't because of all the

problems that came about, the school district would have to come up with the additional money to pay for that podium.

DUTTON: Well, now, from what we've heard from the people that we've interviewed, the question arises: Why was certificates of participation money spent for building the parking facility for retail and for the retail? That's the question that keeps popping up all the time.

SHAMBRA: It wasn't to build the parking for the retail because the retail hadn't come in yet.

DUTTON: But wasn't the developer going to pay for the retail?

SHAMBRA: That was under negotiation.

DUTTON: Oh, it was never consummated?

SHAMBRA: It was never consummated. It was under negotiation. You had to build the podium. The school couldn't sit on air. Somebody had to pay for the air.

According to Mr. Shambra, the structure (the podium) was the platform on which the school would be built. The use of the space under the podium was under negotiation. And because retail contracts were never consummated, there was no problem with using COPs for the construction.

As always, Mr. Shambra was dancing around the truth. The retail component was intended from the very start. According to the revised IRS Preliminary Determination findings:

The developer selection process, which was conducted by Mr. Shambra, David Cartwright, and Wayne Wedin, was specifically decided by the feasibility of having retail facilities as part of the Belmont Learning Complex. In fact, the three developers who were approved to provide Requests for Proposal were instructed to include a retail component in their designs. And even though the lower construction bids came from Goldrich Kest ($58 million) and CRSS/Telacu ($68 million), the decision to go with Temple Beaudry Partners ($98 million) was because of their willingness to include the retail component.

According to Mr. Cartwright, the other developers were not recommended because of their lack of commitment to the retail component:

> "We... We told them specifically that the absence of financial commitment and, thus the putting of the risk of the non-school portion on the District was the fatal flaw for both of the other proposals. If the District is going to take risk on housing and retail, my guess is Mr. Shambra is going to get a...going to have a very difficult time with the State getting money. And the presence of the Kajima guarantee for those portions of the project was, if not the most, one of the three or four most important reasons why the District's team selected them out of the three."

The "Kajima guarantee," referred to by Mr. Cartwright, never materialized. There was no guarantee written in the Disposition and Development Agreement, which required Temple Beaudry Partners to provide retail financing. It was always subject to negotiation.

But the retail component wasn't merely "subject to negotiation." In constructing the podium, the prospective needs of the retailers were taken into account. For example, for the prospective Ralph's supermarket, structural columns were placed to provide adequate aisle space. Even though it later claimed ignorance, LAUSD engaged a leasing agent to lease the retail space. That leasing agent secured tenant lease agreements for the school district's approval. The prospective retail tenants were expected to pay for their own improvements to the retail space, but LAUSD did not ask or require the prospective tenants to contribute to the cost of building the facility.

LAUSD was very concerned about the illegal use of COPs. After the COPs were issued and when the project was being constructed, CFO Henry Jones sent a memorandum to Ray Rodriguez (who reported directly to Dominic Shambra) in which he stated he had learned through a local newspaper that a retail facility was still being constructed as part of the learning complex. When Mr. Jones received no response to his first memorandum, he issued a second memorandum warning there could be no retail construction using the tax-exempt funds from the Certificates of Participation.

Too late. As reports regarding the scandal in Los Angeles reached the East Coast, the IRS looked at the situation and was not pleased. On September 28, 2001, Derek Knight of the Internal Revenue Service in Washington D.C. sent a letter to Joseph Zeronian, then-current Chief Financial Officer for LAUSD. In chilling bureaucrat-eeze he wrote:

> "This is to inform you that we have made a preliminary determination that the interest paid on the Bond Issue named above [$91,400,000 Variable COP's for the Belmont Learning Center] is not excludable from gross income under section 103 of the Internal Revenue Code."

The school district was furious. They quickly hired the most powerful law firm they could find: Sidley Austin Brown & Wood of San Francisco to intercede on their behalf. The IRS wasn't impressed. IRS agent Jack Ferguson sent a short cryptic letter back to Cliff Gerber of Sidley Austin. Among a few clarified statements of document sent and received was this gem:

"All other conditions listed in the September 28, 2001 cover letter remain in effect."

In other words: "Go pound sand."

Somehow the exemption was reinstated. Leslie Dutton pursued this issue in her interview with Dominic Shambra:

SHAMBRA: Now, there was a second letter that came that said that this was not the case.

DUTTON: Yes, I have this.

SHAMBRA: -- that said, this was not the case.

DUTTON: No, not the second letter.

SHAMBRA: That it wasn't used for what the purposes were.

DUTTON: No, the second letter said that the first letter is still in force and that penalties apply. It says right here. "In addition, the examination findings seem to indicate a deliberate attempt to provide misleading valuations and statements that could be considered in addressing any issue of liability for IRC penalties."

SHAMBRA: There was a subsequent letter that said that they dropped the whole issue.

Amazingly he was right.

Ms. Dutton filed Freedom of Information Act requests to every entity involved. After being rebuffed for supposed privacy issues, she finally received on June 16, 2004, a fax from Terry McConville, the LAUSD Director of Litigation Research. Included in this fax was a copy of Agreement with the IRS, a copy of the LAUSD press release, and a copy of the Closed Session Order of Business and minutes from September 24, 2002 where:

> The Board approved entering into a settlement agreement with the Internal Revenue Service (IRS) related to the Certificates of Participation issued in connection with the Belmont Learning Complex, which involves no payment by the District and finding by the IRS that the bonds were and remain non-taxable to their owners.

The vote was seven ayes.

Because the retail component – no matter how intrinsic it was to the whole project – had never materialized: no crime. No penalty. No foul.

No way! According to Special Assistant District Attorney Patchett, California State law was violated when the school district used tax-exempt bonds (COPs)for construction of buildings designed for retail. As he said in his Full Disclosure Network interview:

> "This is how they were finally able to escape from the grasp of IRS that LAUSD indicated that they had never put in a retail structure in there. 'We put a frame in there. So now what we're going to do is to build exclusively a school.'
>
> "I say if you're going to build exclusively a school, you've violated the law because you didn't give the

contract to the lowest bidder. They ended giving it to the highest bidder. The highest bid was $95 million. And it's on its way to half a billion dollars."

But the state Attorney General didn't pursue this allegation. Neither did the Los Angeles County District Attorney. There remains a question of WHY.

And so, the LAUSD School Board finally in 2002 breathed a sigh of relief and put the IRS issue to rest. But in the thick of the fight, the future for the bonds was uncertain. Perhaps the school district could depend on the Proposition BB Bond Oversight Committee to steer things in the right direction.

No way.

CHAPTER 15

The Highest Bidder Wins

As originally conceived, the Belmont Learning Complex was intended to alleviate the severe student overcrowding on a 35-acre site immediately west of downtown Los Angeles. The Belmont project applied a "mixed-use" concept, which included plans for educational, residential, community, and commercial uses. Belmont would have the following components:

- A modern senior high school campus for up to 3,550 students on a regular school year and up to 5,150 students on a year-round calendar basis;
- Up to 125 affordable housing units;
- Up to 27,000 square feet of community facilities, potentially including childcare, youth center, medical clinic, or other community uses; and
- Up to 78,700 square feet of retail facilities, possibly including a supermarket, drugstore, or other similar purposes.

In addition to a mixed-use concept, the LAUSD used a "design-build" bidding process where qualified bidders submitted their own solutions to meet what were only broad LAUSD design parameters.

Advocates of the design-build approach claim various benefits over the more traditional "design-bid-build" method, in which the lowest bid is selected from qualified builders bidding on the same exact design. Design-build is believed to be faster and less costly and is thought to promote creative results.

The mixed-use concept and the design-build approach together added significant complexity to the Belmont project. These strategies required additional and extraordinary expertise, which became increasingly evident that the LAUSD was lacking.

Dominic Shambra created an evaluation team of consultants, who had actual or perceived conflicts, to select a single developer who would then enter exclusive negotiations with the LAUSD to build the Belmont project. Mr. Shambra didn't see the conflicts as a concern – it was the LAUSD doing business as usual. Either waive the conflict or just keep moving forward.

The procurement process included potential developers submitting their proposals, which highlighted their mixed-use and design-build experience along with their project approach and project economics, financing, and suggested revenue to the LAUSD.

The evaluation process consisted of an initial meeting, the preparation of summary reports on each response, and separate, individual interviews with the responding development teams. This information was then used to analyze the responses according to the criteria established in a "Project Evaluation Matrix." The evaluation matrix consisted of the following three main categories which divided up a theoretical total of 100 points:

- Category A (30 points) including, project understanding, project approach, work relationship with District and City, compliance with identified school and community service goals;

- Category B (20 points) including, the achievement of District goals, minority participation, community involvement, jobs created, compliance with RFP requirements; and

- Category C (50 points), including project economics, market research, feasibility, project financing, and suggested revenue to the District.

As you can see, Category C (50% of score) was a key component for potential developers. Category C was basically the retail component associated with the Belmont Learning Complex.

On May 23, 1995, an "evaluation" meeting was conducted to compare the respective scoring of individual members of the evaluation team. The members' scores for each developer were:

Evaluation Team

Member	TBP*	CRSS/Telacu	Goldrich Kest
Mr. Cartwright	86	80	76
Gooden	88	87	76
Mr. Valenzuela	89	83	75

*Temple Beaudry Partners

The evaluation team "unanimously" recommended the selection of Temple Beaudry Partners to enter exclusive negotiations with the LAUSD to reach agreement on the terms of a contract (also referred to as a "Disposition and Development Agreement"). The winning proposal was the most expensive of the three proposals submitted to the District. Dominic Shambra called it the "Cadillac" among the three competitors.

Temple Beaudry Partners	$98 million
CRSS/TELACU	$68 million
Goldrich Kest & Associates	$59 million

In October 1995, the LAUSD and Temple Beaudry Partners began their exclusive negotiations to reach agreement on a contract. In April 1997, an agreement was reached to develop and construct the Belmont Learning Complex. The agreed-to contract established an Overall Fixed Development Price of **$110,410,500**, composed of the following components:

- School and School Parking: $85,875,800
- Contingent Elements: $13,503,000
- Retail Component: $11,031,700 (includes Retail Parking).

The price shown for each of the above components represented a "Guaranteed Maximum Price." Specifically, the "School Component" was composed of the "basic school" with parking; the "Contingent Elements" included an outdoor swimming pool, additional lighting, elements for a joint powers agreement with the City of Los Angeles, etc.); and the "Retail Component" included commercial facilities, such as a grocery store, pharmacy, and other retail outlets.

So, LAUSD seemingly had contracted for a high school at Belmont for the "guaranteed maximum price" of **$85,875,800**. And, today we are talking about a final cost from $400 million to $1 billion. So much for a guaranteed maximum price.

It is important to note that the guaranteed maximum price was (as the term suggests) the Guaranteed Maximum Price. Thus, in the event cost savings were realized, LAUSD stood to receive 70% to 80% of the benefit of a reduction in the total cost of the school. For this reason, it was prudent business practice (or common sense) for the LAUSD staff to review each contractor payment request to make sure that the costs were reasonable and allowable. However, David Cartwright of O'Melveny & Myers advised LAUSD to relax its standard invoice oversight function. This was shocking! Specifically, in a memorandum, dated December 9, 1998, outside counsel cartwright wrote to several LAUSD staff:

> "Because the overall construction price is substantially controlled by the guaranteed maximum price feature, there is less reason for the District to perform an intensive review of the invoice documentation behind the payment request when the line item is a hard guaranteed number."

What?!? No, Mr. Cartwright, you didn't just tell the LAUSD staff to relax their oversight of the payment requests! Yes, he did.

CHAPTER 16

Financial Mismanagement – Belmont was Handled Differently

The LAUSD Chief Financial Officer (CFO) could not answer the fundamental question: "How much has LAUSD spent on Belmont?"

How could that be? A multi-billion dollar organization does not know or could not track dollars spent on the most highly-visible and controversial school construction project it had ever undertaken. What we learned was that this "accounting chaos" was not limited to only the Belmont project. Rather than erring by maintaining the proverbial "two sets of books," LAUSD had an array of accounting methods that collectively did not add up to a single generally accepted set of books.

Throughout our investigation, we were repeatedly told that "Belmont was handled differently" than all other capital projects undertaken by the LAUSD. This was the response, whether we were trying to track the budget or money spent on the project.

During our analysis of the funds spent on Belmont, several systemic issues were identified, such as management officials overriding controls. While these issues may not necessarily relate to the Belmont project alone, they demonstrated severe weaknesses in the LAUSD's financial control systems and gave us little confidence in any information generated by the systems. Some examples of the systemic issues included:

- <u>Direct Payments</u>. LAUSD's financial system had a control feature that required a reference to a contract or a purchase order when posting a payment to a vendor. The purpose of this control was to reduce the risk of overpayment or unauthorized payments. However, an override could be performed in the system by management officials to circumvent this control feature, allowing what is referred to as a "Direct Payment."

If an override was performed on a contract allowing a Direct Payment to a vendor, the contract should have been reduced by the amount of the Direct Payment to prevent an overpayment. This was not always the case. We found that Direct Payments were prevalent in the financial system, which caused three alarming situations –

1. Overpayment of contracts,
2. $77.8 million unnecessarily tied up for years,
3. Large numbers of vendors and jumbo dollar amounts were paid using Direct Payments to vendors.

More troubling was that we found some vendors were paid both by Direct Payments as well as being paid against a contract or purchase order. To site a couple:

<u>O'Melveny & Myers</u>
Direct Payments $6,045,376
Contract Payments $2,930,850
<u>Ernst & Young</u>
Direct Payments $ 709,573
Contract Payments $1,398,669

This practice allowed the LAUSD staff to circumvent system controls for vendor payments and exceed budgets. It also limited anyone's ability to track payments through the computer system and opened wide the door for waste and even fraud.

- Outstanding Encumbrances. The word "encumbrance" is an accounting term used when funds are set aside for a specific contract or purchase order. In a budgetary accounting system such as the LAUSD's, expenditure estimates in the annual budget are appropriated by category and should constitute the maximum expenditures authorized during the fiscal year. These maximums cannot be exceeded unless amended. When a contract is accepted, or a purchase order is issued, a commitment has effectively been made against the budget, and the funds are encumbered against those appropriations, thus reducing the remaining amount available for future expenditures. When Direct Payments are made to a vendor and not applied against the outstanding contract or purchase order, the funds in the budget have essentially been tied up twice.

During our investigation, we discovered outstanding encumbrances of $77.8 million for a six-year period. These were funds reserved in fund balances for subsequent year expenditures. However, because in many instances these contracts were completed by way of Direct Payments, most of these funds were not spent even though these funds were essential for other high priority needs in the school system.

LAUSD's Head Accountant acknowledged that old encumbrances were a problem, but he did not realize they totaled more than $77 million until we informed him. Perhaps more troubling was that the LAUSD's Director of General Accounting also acknowledged the outstanding encumbrance problem, but he was not surprised at the amount that we found and did NOT consider it a big problem.

The outstanding encumbrances amount continued to grow each year and represented another serious weakness with the internal controls associated the LAUSD's financial systems. These types of vulnerabilities allow for overpayments to vendors and kept money set aside that, again, could have otherwise been spent on high priority needs within the school system.

- Miscellaneous Vendors. During our review of vendors, we discovered more than 20 miscellaneous identification codes that could be used to pay vendors. More disturbing, we found that actual payments made to these miscellaneous codes totaled $71.1 million and included payments to more than 10,000 vendors. Payments made to these codes ranged from $1 to $5.4 million.

   While the use of miscellaneous identification codes is not abnormal in practice, the frequency and high dollar values used in the Belmont project dramatically raised a red flag. Abuse of the vendor codes increased the chances of fictitious vendors, duplicate payments, competitive bidding policies not being followed, and inability to track vendor history.

- Budget Transfers. While reviewing the Capital Projects Funds, we discovered that the Facilities Services Division made individual budget transfers for $49,999 on 48 separate occasions between major categories within a specific Fund.

According to the LAUSD's School Board policy, management had the authority to make routine transfers of budget appropriations between major categories within a Fund for no more than $50,000. Transfers greater than $50,000 required School Board approval.

As we repeatedly found during our review of the LAUSD's financial systems and procedures, once again the LAUSD circumvented internal controls. Repeated transfers just below the approved limit raised the question of what was the LAUSD staff trying to hide from the School Board?

In addition to these systemic issues, we also found that it was nearly impossible to follow a trail of accountability through LAUSD's financial accounting systems and processes. For an organization with a multi-billion dollar budget, these types of examples are rarely found.

- The accounting staff kept a double system of bookkeeping records – a "manual record of payment" and a computerized record. The LAUSD staff told us that they didn't trust the computer system.
- The accounts payable files were a disaster. They differed in basic content from vendor to vendor. Sometimes copies of contracts and purchase orders were found, sometimes not. Sometimes original invoices were found, sometimes not. Sometimes copies of invoices were found, sometimes not. Sometimes approvals from appropriate managers were present, sometimes not.
- The accounting for legal services was especially problematic. Attorneys billed for Belmont project work under a "General Counsel" agreement and they also charged for other matters

under the Belmont project contract. Many invoices from attorneys were impossible to track yet approved for payment by the LAUSD General Counsel. For example, an invoice from O'Melveny & Myers was found in disarray in the Accounts Payable files. Four of the projects on the invoice had no purchase order but were approved for payment anyway.

- On invoices and supporting documents, there were signatures and initials that were illegible or unidentifiable and had neither a printed or stamped name or title with them. There were some with signatures, but no dates.
- Changes to vendor invoices were made by including a handwritten memo in the file without identifying who made the changes.

Our detailed analysis of the Belmont project was a dramatic illustration of the dysfunctional culture of the financial management embodied throughout the School District, all the way from the top to the bottom. Although the LAUSD staff wanted to believe that the Belmont saga was unique, these financial management problems and failures had existed at LAUSD for many years. We found that the entire LAUSD financial system could not be relied upon, not just for the Belmont project, but also as it attempted to meet the challenges of its day-to-day operations.

So, I will leave you with this thought – when the LAUSD staff reports that the Belmont project costs were ONLY $400 million, do you believe them?

CHAPTER 17

Cloudy Judgment

"Wisdom is knowing the right path to take. . .
Integrity is taking it."

-M.H. McKee

I once read that "The Rule of Law" was never intended to be the maximum standard of behavior – it's the minimum standard. It's what we <u>can</u> do, not what we <u>should</u> do. But so often, I've found that organizations and their key leaders ask their attorneys, "what can we do?" regarding a specific issue or concern. The better question, however, would be, "what should we do?"

Within the LAUSD, there was a history of nepotism, favoritism, cronyism, and self-dealing. One only needed to look inside the internal audit office that I inherited in January 1999. Shortly after my arrival, I was surprised to learn that members of my audit staff were routinely conducting audits of LAUSD offices or programs where the auditors' relatives (spouses, children, etc.) were either the person in charge of or held a key position within, that office or program. This was a clear violation of the professional auditing standards for independence. The auditors should have recused themselves from performing these audits. But apparently, no one saw this as a problem because it had been happening for at least 30 years. I immediately implemented procedures and a process to eliminate these types of independence issues going forward.

As part of our Belmont investigation, one of our steps was to examine relationships among key players associated with the Belmont project. Based on what I had found in my own office, I wasn't too surprised by some of the questionable behaviors and relationships that we found during our investigation. What did surprise me and our team, however, was how most of the individuals could have recused themselves from their specific conflicts, but did not do so because they either didn't consider their behavior or relationship a technical violation of some law or regulation or it was the way business had always been done at the LAUSD.

I want to give you a few examples that we found which were documented and well known to most of the LAUSD's key leadership, including the School Board, Superintendent, and General Counsel. Ask yourself, were these examples handled appropriately? Often, the *appearance* of unethical behavior is just as important and troubling as actual legal violations.

- Dominic Shambra was appointed the Director of the Office of Planning and Development by then-LAUSD Superintendent Bill Anton. Mr. Shambra was the first and only Director of this Office. The Superintendent authorized Mr. Shambra to operate outside the normal reporting relationships. In fact, Mr. Shambra reported directly to Superintendent Anton. This appointment was a surprising career ladder move considering Mr. Shambra's background and qualifications were that of a playground supervisor, and he now was in charge of developing the concept and finding the funding for the most expensive school construction project in the history of the LAUSD – the Belmont Learning Complex. Basically, he was the Superintendent's "front man" for a multi-million dollar school project. You might ask, how could this happen? Well, it's the LAUSD doing business as usual – you see, Mr. Shambra was the best man at Superintendent Anton's wedding.

- Attorney David Cartwright of the law firm O'Melveny & Myers and LAUSD outside counsel on the Belmont project served as a member on Mr. Shambra's evaluation team to recommend a proposed developer who would enter exclusive negotiations to develop the Belmont Learning Complex. Temple Beaudry Partners was ultimately selected by the evaluation team (a Kajima International entity was a principal partner of Temple Beaudry Partners). LAUSD's General Counsel, Rich Mason, informed us that Kajima International and/or one or more corporate subsidiaries was a "$10 million client" of the O'Melveny firm. Mr. Cartwright did disclose this potential conflict to Mr. Mason and the LAUSD School Board. Mr. Cartwright also offered to resign from the Belmont project if requested do so by the School Board. Again, it's the LAUSD doing business as usual – the School Board voted to enter exclusive negotiations with Temple Beaudry Partners and voted to waive any potential conflict regarding O'Melveny & Meyers and Mr. Cartwright.

- Architect Ernesto Vasquez of architectural firm McLarand, Vasquez & Partners, Inc. was retained to assist the LAUSD on the architectural design of Belmont while concurrently competing as the architect for Temple Beaudry Partners, the developer of the Belmont project. Once again, it's the LAUSD doing business as usual.

- Dr. Betty Hanson, while employed by the California Department of Education, was recruited by Dominic Shambra to be a consultant in his Office of Planning and Development. In her previous job, Dr. Hanson had experience with reviewing and approving contaminated sites for potential school construction – something that Mr. Shambra was facing with the Belmont project, and he could use her help in convincing the California politicians to give him funding for the project. Dr. Hanson joined Mr. Shambra's team as a consultant for $125 per hour and was paid over $250,000 for three years. And once again, it's the LAUSD doing business as usual – you see, Dr. Hanson was Mr. Shambra's girlfriend.

- Dominic Shambra retained staff of the accounting firm Ernst & Young's real estate group to assist him on the evaluation team that was reviewing the various proposals from the prospective developers vying for the right to enter exclusive negotiations with LAUSD on the Belmont project. Ernst & Young was doing work at the same time for Kajima in its Dallas and Washington, D.C. office. Kajima was a partner of the developer Temple Beaudry Partners, who was unanimously recommended by the evaluation team for exclusive negotiations for the Belmont project. Ernst & Young disclosed this potential or real conflict of interest to Mr. Shambra. And yet again, it's the LAUSD doing business as usual – you see, Ernst & Young wasn't only an advisor to Mr. Shambra, Ernst & Young was also LAUSD's external auditor, as well as its accountant for LAUSD's financial records that were used to finance the Belmont project.

In each of these examples, the LAUSD leadership had the opportunity to prevent these actual or perceived conflicts from happening. The LAUSD, however, decided that the ends justified the means and what was best for the individuals involved was what was best in each situation. Rather than do the right thing and make an ethical choice, the LAUSD hid behind what was legal or waived the actual or perceived conflicts.

While DA Cooley's Final Investigative Report found no legal conflicts of interest associated with the Belmont project, his report did highlight that the LAUSD should institute formal procedures to avoid circumstances which call into question the propriety of its school development dealings. The report further highlighted that the mandate should go beyond technical compliance with the prohibitions in California's conflict of interest law. The report emphasized that **merely avoiding criminal acts is not enough; the process should avoid even the appearance of favoritism, cronyism, or self-dealing.**

CHAPTER 18

Who's in Charge?

Apparently, no one!

The people that we thought maybe should have been in charge said they weren't – they said that they were all "coordinators" and working on the project together. An effective school construction and modernization program must appoint a project manager for each major construction project, including major maintenance and renovation projects.

On Monday evening, September 13, 1999, then Board President Genethia Hudley-Hayes and I met with Superintendent Ruben Zacarias in his office to give him a heads up regarding the Belmont report and that it was going to be released the following morning. I told Superintendent Zacarias that even though he had taken a "hands-off" approach with the Belmont project, the buck stopped with him. Ms. Hudley-Hayes and I left the meeting, and as we entered the hallway outside of Superintendent Zacarias's office, we looked at each other, and both said, "he's clueless." It was obvious that Superintendent Zacarias did not understand that we were going to report that he was ultimately responsible for the failures of the Belmont project. In fact, we recommended in our report that the School Board should consider Superintendent Zacarias' failure to supervise the Belmont project in a diligent, professional, and competent manner as part of his next scheduled performance evaluation.

The next day at 6:00 a.m., I briefed the School Board in closed session on the results of phase I of our investigation and that a second report would be issued before the yearend that would focus on the financial aspects of the project. I then held a mid-morning press briefing to summarize our findings.

By the time of the press briefing, it apparently had become crystal clear to Superintendent Zacarias that we were holding him ultimately responsible as he had at least read our report's recommendations and heard what I said to the media and public.

Superintendent Zacarias immediately defaulted to the LAUSD's standard culture that had been used for decades – deny, defend, and deflect. Deny there's a problem, defend the status quo, and use public relations spin to deflect criticism. Interestingly, however, he did publicly agree to implement our report's recommendations.

CHAPTER 19

The Indictment That Wasn't

"The Belmont Learning Complex project was a
public works disaster of biblical proportions."

-DA Steve Cooley

In the fall of 1999, my investigative team and I concluded that we
had probable cause to believe that certain acts or omissions by certain
persons or entities may constitute violations of criminal law, and as
a result, I referred these matters to the appropriate law enforcement
agencies, including the Los Angeles County District Attorney (DA),
which was then headed by DA Gil Garcetti. In April 2000, however,
DA Garcetti notified me that no felony violations were found and
declined prosecution.

There was a public outcry that DA Garcetti was not going to
indict or prosecute anyone for what most felt were clear violations of

environmental law and fraud
related to the Belmont project. The
outcry included Steve Cooley, who
was a candidate in the upcoming
election to be the DA of Los
Angeles County. Mr. Cooley was

extremely critical of DA Garcetti's declination of our referral, and one of Mr. Cooley's campaign promises was to root out wrongdoing connected to the Belmont construction project.

In the November 2000 election, Steve Cooley defeated incumbent Gil Garcetti. In January 2001, DA Cooley asked me to come to his office where I met with him and his newly hired Special Assistant, Anthony Patchett. Mr. Patchett was a veteran prosecutor within the DA's Office and had extensive experience in investigating and prosecuting environment crimes. DA Cooley said that he was creating a Belmont Task Force, which Mr. Patchett would lead, and that he wanted me to be a part of the Task Force. He also wanted me to make available to the Task Force some of my investigative staff. I couldn't say yes fast enough!

The Belmont Task Force began its work in February 2001. The Task Force was composed of senior prosecutors and investigators from the DA's Office, representatives from government agencies, and numerous environmental and construction experts. As DA Cooley had requested, I assisted the Task Force along with several members of my staff that had worked under my direction on our earlier investigation of the Belmont project. The members included Roger Carrick, Denny Kohan, Jim Burns, Michael Walt, Norman Wight, and Darwin Wisdom.

The primary mission of the Task Force was to conduct a comprehensive examination of the Belmont project for possible violations of California criminal law in the development or construction of the Belmont Learning Complex. The Task Force issued 140 grand jury subpoenas, interviewed or obtained statements from 343 witnesses and sources, reviewed more than 1,100 banker's boxes of documents and 8,800 pages of building plans, and consulted numerous outside experts and sources.

In July 2001, after five months of intensive investigative work, key members of the Task Force were summoned to a meeting in a conference room next to DA Cooley's office on the 18th floor of the downtown Criminal Courts Building to review the results of the investigation. Just prior to the start of the meeting and before DA Cooley had arrived, Mr. Patchett distributed a 19-page draft indictment ("Summary of Pleading" document) that contained two felony counts of wrongdoing committed by multiple entities involving at least 20 senior individuals at these entities. However, within just a very few minutes (seemed like seconds), everyone in the room was instructed to return the draft document. Most of us in the room did not even have time to read past page one.

We later learned that DA Cooley and his executive staff declined to adopt the proposed indictment. In a Full Disclosure Network interview of DA Cooley by Leslie Dutton, she challenged DA Cooley – "it was my understanding that Mr. Patchett, as head of the ad hoc Belmont Task Force, that he did recommend indictment." DA Cooley immediately responded, "well, no, he didn't. He did not come up with any plausible theory of criminal liability that withstood any sort of scrutiny." Many of us on the Task Force often wondered why DA Cooley would say that Mr. Patchett did not recommend indictment when over 20 Task Force members witnessed Mr. Patchett handout the draft indictment.

As I sit here today holding a copy of the draft indictment that supposedly didn't exist, I often ask myself why didn't DA Cooley just answer Ms. Dutton's question by saying, "yes, there was an indictment drafted, BUT me and my executive team did not find any plausible theory of criminal liability that would withstand any sort of scrutiny." We'll never know why DA Cooley chose not to be truthful.

In the Spring of 2003, almost 18 months after the "indictment that wasn't meeting," DA Cooley asked me to come to his office so he could share with me the outcome of the Belmont Task Force's investigation before he made the results public. I entered Mr. Cooley's office – he sat behind his desk, and I sat in a chair directly across from him. At least two of his executive staff were seated behind me along the back wall of his office. Mr. Cooley thanked me for my support, especially the investigative resources that I provided to the Task Force. Then came the dagger to the heart – we will not be filing any criminal charges because we found no credible evidence of wrongdoing. He went on to say, however, we do plan to issue a report that contains several lessons learned. Once I pulled out the dagger, I said to DA Cooley – no evidence of wrongdoing? What about the subcontractor that admitted to one of my attorneys and me during an interview that his company created false invoices at the direction of the prime contractor? DA Cooley looked surprised, and his eyes turned to his executives along the back wall, and no one said a word. After a short sound of silence, DA Cooley noted that we'd considered all the evidence, and there will not be any charges. He also said that when he does issue the final report, he will hold a press conference and that he would like me to be there and stand beside him to offer my support. I didn't say yes or no – I had heard enough.

On the morning of March 3, 2003, Mr. Cooley held a press conference and released the Final Investigative Report on the Belmont Learning Complex. I'll never forget that morning. I decided to take the day off, stay home, and relax – I had enough of Belmont. My phone was ringing, and it was the Public Affairs Office calling on behalf of DA Cooley asking where I was because the press conference was about to begin, and DA Cooley wanted me there. I told the public affairs person not to wait on me because I won't be there – I hung my phone and enjoyed my day off.

After the press conference, many people were outraged and began to criticize DA Cooley even worse than they had DA Gil Garcetti. Roger Carrick, who served as my special counsel on our Belmont investigation, issued a statement charging DA Cooley with lowering the bar for environmental compliance when it comes to protecting our children and their schools. Mr. Carrick said that "Mr. Cooley should be ashamed of himself. Today Mr. Cooley simply reaffirmed his office's prior whitewash of Belmont."

Anthony Patchett, who headed the Belmont Task Force until DA Cooley removed him in July 2001, was a little more restrained in his comments because DA Cooley had placed a "gag order" on him not to disclose anything he learned during the investigation. Mr. Patchett's only comment was that the DA's report contradicted what was in the LAUSD Inspector General's report and the findings of his investigation. Mr. Patchett also stated that grand jury time had been reserved for presenting the Task Force's findings, but DA Cooley canceled the time.

DA Cooley responded to the outrage by stating that "I know what our office did. I know what the lawyers did in this case. I'm very pleased and proud of what we did." A few months later, while interviewing DA Cooley, Full Disclosure Network host Leslie Dutton asked DA Cooley how could the Inspector General's Belmont report identify so many problems and provide all of these supporting exhibits and your office find nothing wrong?

DA Cooley responded, "Well, there's a lot wrong – the Belmont high school project, the Belmont Learning Center was probably the worst public works disaster perhaps in the history of the country at least in terms of school building – a lot went wrong over there." At least, DA Cooley did comment that the Belmont Learning Complex project was a "public works disaster of biblical proportions."

Even though the cover of the Final Investigative Report showed that it was the product of the Belmont Task Force, the Task Force members did not see the draft or final report before it was made public. Most Task Force members were shocked that the DA did not plan on filing any criminal charges. In fact, Ed Scott, a Task Force member said publicly that although his name and those of other experts were used in the DA's March 2003 Final Investigative Report on Belmont "at no time did anybody from the DA's office ask us to review the findings of this report or ask us to concur with the findings of this report."

Although extremely disappointed in the failure to move forward with any indictments, I was pleased that Chapter 10 of the DA's final report ("Lessons from The Belmont Learning Complex Project") validated the findings from my Belmont report that had been issued over four years earlier.

With the public release of the DA's final investigative report on Belmont, one would think that Belmont was over. But, David Cartwright (the O'Melveny & Myers Partner and LAUSD's outside counsel) felt the urge to confirm that the LAUSD culture of deny, defend and deflect was engrained not only in its internal staff but also in its outside attorney – basically, continue to defend the Belmont project no matter what! This was made very clear during a Full Disclosure Network's interview of Mr. Cartwright when he told host Leslie Dutton that Mullinax's Belmont report was "a work of fiction." Cartwright passionately added that "If you read Cooley's report other than the prologue and the postlude, you will find that not only doesn't it support any charges, it says the Belmont project is a great project."

"... a great project?" Did I hear him correctly? I had to listen to his statement more than once because I kept thinking to myself – he's an attorney of law, and he just lied publicly. If you read DA Cooley's 220-page investigative report, you won't find the words "a great project" anywhere. In fact, the truthful conclusion contained in DA Cooley's final report was that "The Belmont Learning Complex project has been a continuing public tragedy of mistakes, misfortune, missed deadlines, and mishandling of the educational interests of our children."

CHAPTER 20

The Final Chapter – Now What?

No criminal or civil prosecutions and no fines or penalties – only a few removals of LAUSD staff, most of whom came back to work later. So, what did we learn?

Here are 10 key takeaways from my Belmont experience to help school systems and educational institutions that are considering building or renovating facilities:

1) Appoint a project manager for all school construction projects, including significant maintenance and renovation projects.
2) Hire internal staff that has the requisite skills to effectively monitor all aspects of construction projects, including site selection, environmental risk management; contracting methods and strategies; and budgeting, estimating payments, and cost controls.
3) Establish and maintain a program of orientation for new board members as to their responsibilities under applicable laws and school board policies, including school construction and modernization.
4) Promote a culture of excellence through teamwork, open communication, and sharing of information so that the

education institution, as well as the public, are fully aware of key developments, progress, and decisions related to projects.

5) Create an internal oversight group, such as an office of internal audit, office of inspector general, or audit committee.

6) Establish an ethics and conflict of interest policy that is applicable to all employees, as well as consultants, contractors, attorneys, and any other contract employees.

7) Assess and document the adequacy of potential school sites, including all environmental risks and proposed mitigations for those risks.

8) Resolve any environmental safety issues during the project planning phase, including NOT adopting a strategy of "mitigate as needed" or purchasing property "as is."

9) Thoroughly study and adequately evaluate the merits of a "mixed-use concept" and "design-build approach" for any construction projects. If these concepts and approaches are used, hire the management expertise needed to manage appropriately, and oversee this strategy.

10) Establish an appropriate project accounting system that provides useful, relevant, timely, and reliable information to use for oversight and decision-making.

With the publication of this book, my Belmont saga will end. Having lived with the Belmont project for the past 20 years, however, I have many personal takeaways that will continue with me forever – I'll only share three of them with you.

First, the amazing people that I met along the way and lasting relationships that were built will be with me for a lifetime. Second, I often think of the people who were so dedicated to our investigation but are no longer with us, such as Roger Carrick and Mike Walt.

They both gave their hearts and souls to our work. Finally, I couldn't end this book without acknowledging the dedicated citizens of Los Angeles and its surrounding areas who supported me, the Office of Inspector General, and our Belmont investigation. They were there with us through the good and bad times. In the end, all of us wanted what was best for the children of the Belmont community – a safe neighborhood school.

Printed in the United States
By Bookmasters